DAILY READINGS FROM

THE
POWER
OF I AM

Also by Joel Osteen

DAILY READINGS FROM

THE
POWER
OF *I AM*

JOEL OSTEEN

New York • Boston • Nashville

I can do all things...
through Him who strengthens
and empowers me
[...I am self-sufficient
in Christ's sufficiency;
I am ready for anything
and equal to anything
through Him who infuses me
with inner strength
and confident peace.]

PHILIPPIANS 4:13 AMP

INTRODUCTION

Have you wondered if you have inner strengths, natural talents, and unique abilities that will make you prosper with self-assurance and success? Do you want to build the quiet confidence to face any obstacle that comes your way?

My friend, over the next 365 days, I'd like for you to take the journey of a lifetime together with me and explore a simple yet profound principle that can help you answer those questions and attain your dreams and goals. With the words "I am," you can control your success or failure, transform your self-image, invite the right things into your life, and redirect your life's course onto the road of your destiny.

I AM. Can these two words give you the power to change your life? Can they help you discover unique abilities and advantages you never knew you had that can lead to a more productive and happier life? Yes, they can!

Why? Because what follows these two words will determine the course of your life. Whatever follows the words "I am" will always come looking for you. So when you go through the day saying, "I am blessed," blessings pursue you. When you say, "I am healthy," health heads your way. When you say, "I am strong," strength tracks you down. That is life-changing!

The reason I've written this devotional is to help you harness *The Power of I Am* and become who God made you to be—an amazing, original masterpiece chosen by the Most High God to do great things. You'll learn powerful "I am"s for your life that will provide you with practical steps and encouragement for creating a life without limitations. It's time to stop criticizing yourself and discover an extraordinary life.

I trust that these devotions will inspire you in your daily walk with God. While they are not meant to replace your personal time with God, it is my desire that the readings will be keys you can use to unlock doors leading to a fuller life. I hope they will be a springboard to help you draw nearer to God and to help you overcome the challenges or barriers that might keep you from discovering your best life possible.

Your life can be transformed and renewed as you allow God's Word to refresh and to reshape your thinking, speaking, and daily activities. You will find a wealth of Scriptures and points for contemplation. Allow the Scriptures to speak to your heart. Be still and listen to what God is saying to you. Day by day, the barriers that hold you back will begin to loosen and fall off your life.

No matter what challenges or troubles you face, you can choose to rise to a new level and invite God's goodness into your life by focusing on these two words, I AM!

DAILY READINGS FROM

THE
POWER
OF *I AM*

"I Am"

*A man will be satisfied
with good from the fruit
of his words...*

PROVERBS 12:14 AMP

JANUARY 1

Whether you realize it or not, all through the day the power of "I am" is at work in your life, for what follows those two simple words will determine what kind of life you live. The "I am"s coming out of your mouth will bring either success or failure.

Here's the principle. *Whatever follows the "I am" will always come looking for you.* When you say, "I am so clumsy," clumsiness comes looking for you. "I am so old." Wrinkles come looking for you. "I am so overweight." Calories come looking for you. It's as though you're inviting them. Whatever you follow the "I am" with, you're handing it an invitation, opening the door, and giving it permission to be in your life.

Wield the Power

By the grace of God I am what I am,
and His grace toward me was not in vain.

1 CORINTHIANS 15:10 NKJV

Many times we wield the power of "I am" against ourselves. We don't realize how it's affecting our future. That's why you have to be careful what follows the "I am." Don't ever say, "I am so unlucky all the time." You're inviting disappointments. "I am so broke. I am so in debt." You are inviting struggle. You're inviting lack.

The good news is you get to choose what follows the "I am." When you go through the day saying, "I am blessed," blessings come looking for you. "I am talented." Talent comes looking for you. You may not feel up to par, but when you say, "I am healthy," health starts heading your way. "I am strong." Strength starts tracking you down. You're inviting that into your life.

Invite the Good

My tongue is the pen of a skillful writer.

PSALM 45:1

How many people, when they get up in the morning, look in the mirror, shake their head, and the first thing they say is, "I am so worn out. I am so wrinkled. I am so old." You're inviting fatigue. You are inviting oldness. Do us all a favor; stop inviting that.

You need to send out some new invitations. Get up in the morning and invite good things into your life. "I am blessed. I am strong. I am talented. I am wise. I am disciplined. I am focused. I am prosperous." When you talk like that, talent gets summoned by Almighty God: "Go find that person." Health, strength, abundance, and discipline start heading your way, and it costs you nothing!

Beautiful

Dark am I, yet lovely,
daughters of Jerusalem...

SONG OF SOLOMON 1:5

Some people have never once said, "I am beautiful. I am attractive." They're so focused on their flaws and what they don't like about themselves and how they wish they had more here and less there. When you say, "I am beautiful," beauty comes looking for you. Youth and freshness come looking for you. Nobody else can do this for you! It has to come out of your own mouth.

Not only that, but on the inside your spirit person comes alive. Your self-image begins to improve, and you'll start carrying yourself like you're someone special. You won't drag around feeling inferior. Beauty is not in how thin or tall you are, how perfect you look. Beauty is in being who God made you to be with confidence.

God's Creation

"Before I formed you in the womb I knew you, before you were born I set you apart..."

JEREMIAH 1:5

Don't go around telling others how negative you feel about yourself, whether about your looks or personality. Never put yourself down, especially not in front of your spouse. The last thing they need to hear is how bad you think you look. Don't put those negative thoughts in their minds.

God made you as you are on purpose. He gave you your looks, your height, your skin color, your nose, your personality. Nothing about you is by accident. You didn't get overlooked. You didn't get left out. God calls you His masterpiece. Instead of going around feeling down on yourself, too tall, too short, not enough of this, or too much of that, dare to say, "I am a masterpiece. I am created in the image of Almighty God."

Amazing and Wonderful

I praise you because you made me in an amazing and wonderful way. What you have done is wonderful.

PSALM 139:14 NCV

Notice David's "I am"s. He was saying, not in pride but in praise to God, "I am wonderful. I am amazing. I am a masterpiece." That goes against human nature. Most of us think, *There's nothing amazing about me. Nothing wonderful. I'm just average. I'm just ordinary.* But the fact is there is nothing ordinary about you. There will never be another you. Even if you have an identical twin, somebody who looks exactly like you, they don't have your same personality, your same goals, or even your same fingerprints. You are an original. When God made you, He threw away the mold. But as long as you go around thinking, *I'm just average. There's nothing special about me,* the wrong "I am" will keep you from rising higher.

Called by Your Name

But now, thus says the Lord, who created you, O Jacob, and He who formed you, O Israel: "Fear not, for I have redeemed you; I have called you by your name; you are Mine."

ISAIAH 43:1 NKJV

Rather than being down on ourselves and focusing on all our flaws, all through the day—not in front of other people but in privacy, driving to work, and underneath our breath—be as bold as David was and say, "I am amazing. I am wonderful. I am valuable. I am a masterpiece. I am a child of the Most High God!" You talk like that and amazing comes chasing you down. Awesome starts heading in your direction. You won't have that weak, defeated, "I'm just average" mentality. You'll carry yourself like a king, like a queen. Not in pride. Not being better than somebody, but with a quiet confidence, with a knowing that you've been handpicked by the Creator of the universe and you have something amazing to offer this world.

Royalty

"As for Sarai your wife, you are no longer to call her Sarai; her name will be Sarah.... I will bless her so that she will be the mother of nations; kings of peoples will come from her."

GENESIS 17:15–16

God promised Sarai and her husband, Abram, that they would have a baby. But Sarai was eighty years old, way past the childbearing years. Back in those days, if a wife couldn't conceive and give her husband a child, she was considered to be a failure. I can imagine some of her "I am"s: "I am a failure. I am inferior to other women. I am not good enough."

God knew that the promise of a child would never come to pass unless He could convince Sarai to change her "I am"s. It was so imperative that she have this new mind-set that God actually changed her name from *Sarai* to *Sarah*, which means "Princess." Helping Sarah move from "I am a failure" to "I am a Princess" changed everything!

Reign in Life

*...how much more will those who receive
God's abundant provision of grace and
of the gift of righteousness reign in life
through the one man, Jesus Christ!*

ROMANS 5:17

When God changed Sarai's name to Sarah, which means "Princess," she heard this spoken to her over and over. Those words got on the inside and began to change her self-image. Sarah went from "I am ashamed" to "I am crowned by Almighty God." Instead of hanging her head in defeat, she started holding her head up high. From "I'm not good enough" to "I am a child of the Most High God." From "I'm inferior" to "I am amazing and wonderfully made." Her new attitude became: *I am a masterpiece.*

This Princess spirit got on the inside of Sarah. It changed her self-image. I've learned you have to change on the inside before you'll see change on the outside. Against all odds, she gave birth to that baby. The promise came to pass.

Your New Name

"No longer will you be called Abram; your name will be Abraham, for I have made you a father of many nations."

GENESIS 17:5

JANUARY

10

As was true for Sarah, you may have had a lot of things in life try to push you down—bad breaks and disappointments, maybe even people who have tried to make you feel as though you just don't measure up or you're not talented enough. You could easily let that seed get on the inside, ruin your sense of value, and cause you to live inferior.

But God is saying to you what He said to Sarai, "I want you to change your name"—not literally, but in your attitude. Shake off the negative things people have said about you and quit telling yourself you're all washed up. Do as Sarah did and say, "I am royalty. I am crowned with favor. I am excited about my future."

Life-Giving Words

*The tongue has the
power of life and death.*

PROVERBS 18:21

Words have creative power. They can be very helpful like electricity. Used the right way, electricity powers lights, air conditioning, and all kinds of good things. But electricity used the wrong way can harm you, even kill you. It's the same way with our words. It's up to you to choose what follows the "I am."

What kind of "I am"s are coming out of your mouth? "I am victorious. I am blessed. I am talented. I am anointed." When you have the right "I am"s, you're inviting the goodness of God. My encouragement is to never say negative things about yourself. That is cursing your future. Do yourself a favor and zip that up. We have enough in life against us already. Don't be against yourself.

January 12

By Faith

God, who gives life to the dead, and calls the things that are not, as though they were.

ROMANS 4:17 WEB

Today's scripture simply means that you shouldn't talk about the way you are. Talk about the way you want to be. If you're struggling in your finances, don't go around saying, "Oh, man, business is so slow. The economy is so down. It's never going to work out." That's calling the things that are as if they will always be that way. That's just describing the situation. By faith you have to say, "I am blessed. I am successful. I am surrounded by God's favor."

The Scripture says, "Let the weak say, 'I am strong!'" (Joel 3:10 AMP)—not the opposite, "I am so tired. I am so rundown." Let the poor say, "I am well off"—not, "I am broke. I am so in debt." Don't call in the wrong things.

God Says So

*The LORD will make you the head,
not the tail.*

DEUTERONOMY 28:13

Have you allowed what somebody—a coach, a teacher, a parent, an ex-spouse—said about you to plant negative seeds of what you cannot do. "You're not smart enough, talented enough, disciplined enough, or attractive enough. You'll always be mediocre and struggle with your weight." Get rid of those lies! That is not who you are. You are who God says you are.

People may have tried to tell you who or what you can't become. Let that go in one ear and out the other ear. What somebody said about you doesn't determine your destiny; *God does.* You need to know not only who you are but also who you are not. In other words, "I am not who people say I am. I am who God says I am."

No Intimidation

Don't be intimidated in any way by your enemies.

PHILIPPIANS 1:28 NLT

You have gifts and talents that you've not tapped into yet. There is a treasure on the inside. Negative thoughts will try to keep it buried. The enemy doesn't want you to reach your full potential. There are forces constantly trying to make you feel intimidated, inferior, unqualified. If you're going to fulfill your destiny, you have to shake off the negative voices.

Shake off the thoughts that are telling you, *I am unable. I am unqualified.* Don't invite weakness. Don't give intimidation an invitation. Before you were born, God equipped you. He empowered you. You are not lacking anything. When you know God has approved you, you realize, *I don't need other people's approval. I've been equipped, empowered, and anointed by the Creator of the universe!*

Change Your "I Am"

*Surely, LORD, you bless the
righteous; you surround them with
your favor as with a shield.*

PSALM 5:12

I know a man who was told by a counselor
that he wasn't very smart and should
focus on the lowest skilled factory job that
he could find, which he did. Years later,
he was hired at another factory where he
was given an IQ test that assessed him at a
genius level. He went on to start his own
business, and he invented and patented two
very successful products.

What happened? He changed his "I am."
Could it be what someone has told you is
keeping you from God's best? Do what this
man did. Change your "I am." Get in agreement with God and declare who you are
and know who you are not. "I am not lacking. I am not inferior. I am equipped. I am
empowered."

Be on Guard

*They gave Moses this account:
"We went into the land to
which you sent us, and it does
flow with milk and honey!
Here is its fruit. But..."*

NUMBERS 13:27–28

In Numbers 13, Moses sent twelve men
in to spy out the Promised Land. After
forty days, ten of them came back and said,
"Moses, we don't have a chance. The cities
are fortified and very large and the people
are huge. Compared to them we felt like we
were grasshoppers." Notice their "I am"s. "I
am weak. I am inferior. I am intimidated. I
am afraid." What happened? Fear, intimidation, and inferiority came knocking at
the door.

What is interesting is that the negative
report from the ten spies spread like wild-
fire throughout the rest of the camp. Before
long some two million people were intimidated and afraid. When people are murmur-
ing, complaining, and talking defeat, be on
guard. Make sure you don't let the wrong "I
am" take root.

Be a Joshua

*"...don't be afraid of the people
of the land. They are only help-
less prey to us! They have no
protection, but the LORD is with
us! Don't be afraid of them!"*

NUMBERS 14:9 NLT

In Numbers 13, ten men sent to spy out
the Promised Land brought back a negative report. The other two spies, Joshua and
Caleb, said, "Moses, yes, the people are big,
but we know our God is much bigger. We
are well able. Let us go in and take the land
at once." Their "I am"s were just the opposite. "I am strong. I am equipped. I am confident. I am more than a conqueror."

But nobody in the camp even paid
attention to Joshua and Caleb's report of
faith. Don't let that be your destiny. You
may be facing some major obstacles. My
challenge is for you to be a Joshua. Be a
Caleb. "I am well able." Make sure you have
the right "I am"s coming out of your mouth.

Be Very Careful

"So tell them, 'As surely as I live, declares the LORD, I will do to you the very thing I heard you say...'"

NUMBERS 14:28

The people of Israel were so distressed by the negative report of the ten spies that they complained against Moses and Aaron, "Why did you even bring us out here? We're going to die in the wilderness. Our children, our wives, they're going to be taken as plunder."

God answered back something very powerful and very sobering. He said in Numbers 14, "I will do for you exactly what you have said. You said you're going to die in the wilderness, so you will die in the wilderness." God is saying the same thing to us. "I am going to do exactly what you've been saying." Don't ever say, "I am weak. I'm intimidated. I'm inferior." Friend, the wrong "I am" can keep you from your destiny.

Seeds of Greatness

"But because my servant Caleb has
a different spirit and follows me wholeheartedly,
I will bring him into the land he went to,
and his descendants will inherit it."

NUMBERS 14:24

In the Scripture, do you remember reading about a man named Sethur, a man named Gaddi, or a man named Shaphat? I'm fairly certain that you've never heard of them. You know why? They were listed among the ten spies who brought the negative report. They also never made it into the Promised Land. The fact is they were called to be history makers, just as Joshua and Caleb were. They had seeds of greatness on the inside, but the wrong "I am" kept them from making their mark.

Joshua and Caleb were the only two people who were twenty years old and above from that whole wilderness company to ever make it into the Promised Land.

A Fountain of Life

The mouth of the righteous is a fountain of life and his words of wisdom are a source of blessing...

PROVERBS 10:11 AMP

JANUARY

20

Here are some "I am"s to speak over your life every day. Get them down in your spirit. Meditate on them. They may not all be true right now, but as you continue to speak them, they will become a reality.

"I am valuable. I am redeemed. I am forgiven. I am approved. I am successful. I am victorious. I am talented. I am healthy. I am energetic. I am happy. I am positive. I am passionate. I am strong. I am confident. I am secure. I am attractive. I am free. I am qualified. I am motivated. I am focused. I am determined. I am patient. I am kind. I am generous. I am empowered. I am well able. I am a child of the Most High God."

Words Are Like Seeds

*Keep your tongue
from evil and your lips
from speaking deceit.*

PSALM 34:13 AMP

You are where you are today in part because of what you've been saying about yourself. Words are like seeds. When you speak something out, you give life to what you're saying. If you continue to say it, eventually that can become a reality. Whether you realize it or not, you are prophesying your future. This is great when you're saying things such as, "I'm blessed. I will accomplish my dreams. I'm coming out of debt." That's not just being positive; you are actually prophesying victory and new levels.

But too many people go around prophesying just the opposite. "I never get any good breaks." "I'll probably get laid off." They don't realize they are prophesying defeat. Your life will move in the direction of your words.

Abundant Fruit

Death and life are in the power of the tongue,
and those who love it and indulge it will eat its fruit
and bear the consequences of their words.

PROVERBS 18:21 AMP

The Scripture says, "We will eat the fruit of our words." When you talk, you are planting seeds. At some point, you're going to eat that fruit. My challenge is: Make sure you're planting the right kind of seeds. If you want apples, you have to sow apple seeds. If you want oranges, you can't plant cactus or poison ivy seeds. You're going to reap fruit from the exact seeds that you've been sowing.

If you don't like what you're seeing, start sowing some different seeds. Instead of saying, "I'll never get well," plant the right seeds by stating, "God is restoring health back to me. This sickness didn't come to stay; it came to pass." You keep sowing those positive seeds and eventually you'll eat that abundant fruit—health, wholeness, victory.

Speak the Promises

"If you want to enjoy life and see many happy days, keep your tongue from speaking evil and your lips from telling lies."

1 PETER 3:10 NLT

You can't talk negative and expect to live a positive life. You can't talk defeat and expect to have victory. If you talk lack, not enough, can't afford it, and never get ahead, you're going to have a poor life.

Instead of saying, "I'll never get out of debt. I'll never rise any higher," you start speaking the promises of God: "I will lend and not borrow. Whatever I touch prospers and succeeds. I'm coming into overflow, into more than enough." Start sowing seeds of increase, seeds of abundance. No more "I'll never accomplish my dreams." Instead, "I have the favor of God. The right people are searching me out. New opportunities, new levels are in my future." If you'll keep talking like that, you'll reap a harvest of good things.

Bless Your Life

And so blessing and cursing come pouring out of the same mouth. Surely, my brothers and sisters, this is not right!

JAMES 3:10 NLT

Many people don't realize that every time they say, "I never get any good breaks," they just cursed their life. "I'll never be able to afford a house." "I'll never be able to break this addiction." "I'll never meet the right person." Sometimes the enemy doesn't have to defeat us; we defeat ourselves. Pay attention to what you're saying. Are you blessing your life? Or are you cursing it?

I've known guys who joke about how they are getting old, fat, and bald, and fifteen years later it came true. Don't speak that defeat over your life. Our attitude should be, *God is renewing my youth like the eagles. I'm getting stronger, healthier, better looking. I'm going to live a long productive faith-filled life.* Start blessing your life. Prophesy good things.

You Will Prevail

"No weapon forged against you will prevail, and you will refute every tongue that accuses you. This is the heritage of the servants of the LORD..."

ISAIAH 54:17

I know a man who was only in his early fifties and yet was so concerned he was going to get Alzheimer's disease that he was actually making plans for someone to take care of him. Of course, it's good to be wise and to plan ahead in your life where you can, but if you're making plans to get a disease, you probably won't be disappointed. You're sending it an invitation.

I told him what I'm telling you, "Start declaring, 'No weapon formed against me will ever prosper. I will live out my days in good health, with a clear mind, with a good memory, with clarity of thought. My youth is being renewed.'" You must prophesy health. Prophesy a long productive life. Your words will become your reality.

Don't Be Snared

You are snared by the words of your mouth; you are taken by the words of your mouth.

PROVERBS 6:2 NKJV

To be *snared* means "to be trapped." Your words can trap you. What you say can cause you to stumble and keep you from your potential. You're not snared by what you think. Negative thoughts come to us all. But when you speak them out, you give them life. That's when they become a reality.

If you say, "I'll never get back in shape," it becomes more difficult. When you say, "I never get any good breaks," that stops the favor that was ordained to you. If you say, "I'm not that talented. I don't have a good personality," that is calling in mediocrity. It's setting the limits for your life. When negative thoughts come, the key is to never verbalize them. That thought will die stillborn if you don't speak it.

Prophesy the Right Thing

JANUARY 27

The heart of the wise teaches his mouth, and adds learning to his lips.

PROVERBS 16:23 NKJV

When we acquired the former Compaq Center, it was a dream come true. We were so excited...and then our architects told us it was going to cost 100 million dollars to change it from a basketball arena to a church! My first thoughts were, *That's impossible! I can't raise those kinds of funds.*

Even though those thoughts were racing through my mind, I knew enough to keep my mouth closed. I told our team, "God has a way. He didn't bring us this far to leave us. He is supplying all our needs. The funds are coming in. It may look impossible on paper, but with God all things are possible." I knew if I kept prophesying the right things, we would start moving toward it, and we did!

Talk about the Promise

Those who control their tongue will have a long life;
opening your mouth can ruin everything.

PROVERBS 13:3 NLT

In the tough times, it's very tempting to vent your frustration and tell people how the loan didn't go through, how bad the medical report was, or how certain people just didn't treat you right. When you continually talk about the problem, that's only going to make you more discouraged, and it gives that problem more life. You're making it bigger. Turn it around. Don't talk about the problem; talk about the promise.

Instead of complaining, "I didn't get the promotion they promised," declare, "I know when one door closes that means God has something better." If your friend remarks, "I heard those people did you wrong," feel free to smile and explain, "Yes, but I'm not worried. God is fighting my battles. He's promised to give me beauty for ashes."

The Voice of Faith

A man has joy by the answer of his mouth,
and a word spoken in due season, how good it is!

PROVERBS 15:23 NKJV

In life, there are always two voices competing for your attention—the voice of faith and the voice of defeat. One voice declares that you've reached your limits and don't have what it takes. You'll be tempted to worry, to be negative, to complain. But if you listen carefully, you'll hear another voice saying, "You are well able. You can do all things through Christ. Favor is coming."

Now, you get to choose which voice comes to life. Whichever thought you verbalize is given the right to come to pass. If you say, "The problem's too big," you are choosing the wrong voice. You must get in agreement with God. The other voice may seem louder, but you can override it. You can take away all its power by choosing the voice of faith.

No More Defeat

The mouth of the righteous flows with [skillful and godly] wisdom...

PROVERBS 10:31 AMP

JANUARY

30

Does this sound familiar? You're going to a job interview, and the voice of defeat says, "You're not going to get it. You're wasting your time." But the voice of faith counters, "You have the favor of God. You have what it takes." If you tell your spouse, "I don't think I'm going to get this job," there's no use in going. You're being trapped by your words.

You have to dig your heels in and say, "I am not giving life to any more defeat. I am not speaking lack. I'm not speaking sickness. I'm not speaking mediocrity, fear, or doubt. I'm choosing the voice of faith. It says I am strong, I am healthy, and I am blessed. I am favored. I am a victor and not a victim."

Zip It

"Before I formed you in the womb I knew you, before you were born I set you apart; I appointed you as a prophet to the nations."

JEREMIAH 1:5

God gave Jeremiah a promise that he would become a great prophet to the nations. But when he heard God's voice, he was very young and unsure of himself. He instead listened to the voice of doubt and said, "God, I can't do that. I can't speak to the nations. I'm too young. I wouldn't know what to say."

God said, "Jeremiah, say not that you are too young." The first thing God did was to stop his negative words. Why did God do that? Because He knew that if Jeremiah went around saying, "I'm not qualified. I can't do this. I don't have what it takes," he would become exactly what he was saying. So God said in effect, "Jeremiah, zip it up. You may think it, but don't speak it out."

Stop the Excuses

*May these words of my mouth
and this meditation of my heart
be pleasing in your sight, LORD,
my Rock and my Redeemer.*

PSALM 19:14

When Jeremiah stopped making the excuse that he was too young and changed what he was saying, he became a prophet to the nations. God's promise came to pass.

In the same way, God has called every one of us to do something great. He's put dreams, desires on the inside, but it's easy to acquiesce as Jeremiah did and say, "I can't do that. I'm too young. I'm too old. I've made too many mistakes. I don't have the education. I don't have the experience." We can all make excuses, but God is saying to us what He said to Jeremiah, "Stop saying that." Don't curse your future. Those negative words can keep you from God's best.

A Promise Delayed

Praise the Lord, you angels,
you mighty ones who carry out
his plans, listening for each
of his commands.

PSALM 103:20 NLT

Sometimes the reason a promise from
God is being delayed is because of what
we're saying. Imagine that God has already
dispatched an angel with your healing, your
promotion, your vindication. But en route,
God says to the angel, "Hold on." The angel
replies, "Why? This is what You promised
in Your Word." God answers, "That's right,
but he's talking about how it's not going to
happen."

Negative words stop God's promises.
I wonder how many times we're right on
the brink of seeing the answer. Perhaps
you've been praying for years that God
would bring somebody great into your life.
But right before they show up, you let your
guard down and start saying, "Oh, I'm too
old. Nobody's interested in me." God has to
say to the angel, "Don't go any farther."

Do Your Part

"See, I am doing a new thing! Now it springs up;
do you not perceive it? I am making a way in the
wilderness and streams in the wasteland."

ISAIAH 43:19

The good news is that even if you got negative about a promise from God, He didn't cancel it. He still has the right person for you, and if you'll zip up the doubt and switch over into faith, at the right time, that person will show up. God will release what negative words have delayed. God still has your healing, your promotion, your restoration on hold.

Now do your part. Quit talking about how it's not going to happen. It may look impossible, but God can do the impossible. Just because you don't see anything happening doesn't mean God is not working. Right now, behind the scenes, God is arranging things in your favor. He is positioning you exactly where He wants you to be. Now don't delay the promise by speaking negative words.

Turn It Around

*Trust in the L*ORD *with all your heart
and lean not on your own understanding...*

PROVERBS 3:5

Let's say your son is in the process of applying to different colleges. Some schools only accept five percent of the students who apply. It's easy to think, *Why bother to apply to those schools? More than nine out of ten students get denied. There is no way.*

Don't be snared by the words of your mouth and talk yourself out of it. You may think those thoughts, but don't verbalize them. Learn to turn it around. "God, I know You have my son in the palm of Your hand. There may be only a five percent chance for some schools, but God, I know that with You there's a hundred percent chance he'll get in exactly where You want him to go. God, You control the whole universe." Your words prophesy your future.

Rest Assured

Zechariah asked the angel, "How can I be sure of this? I am an old man and my wife is well along in years."

LUKE 1:18

In Luke 1, an angel appeared to Zechariah and told him that his wife was going to have a baby. Zechariah was very surprised, and he listened to the voice of doubt. He asked the angel, "Are you sure? Do you see how old we are?" The angel said, "I am Gabriel. I stand in the presence of God, and what God says will come to pass."

But God knows the power of our words. He knew that if Zechariah went around speaking defeat, it would stop His plan. So God did something unusual. The angel said, "Zechariah, because you doubted, you will remain silent and not be able to speak until the baby is born." Zechariah couldn't speak one word for nine months. God zipped it for him, lest he lose the promise.

Set a Guard

Set a guard over my mouth, LORD;
keep watch over the door of my lips.

PSALM 141:3

Yesterday we read that God took away Zechariah's speech. God knew he would go out and start telling his friends how it wasn't going to happen. Those negative words would have stopped his destiny. That's why the Scripture says, "Set a watch over your mouth." In other words, "Be careful what you allow to come out of your mouth."

"I'll never pass this algebra course. I've never been good in math." No, put a watch over your mouth. Don't prophesy that defeat. If you're going to say anything, declare what God says, "I can do all things through Christ. I have good understanding. I am full of wisdom. I am an A student." When you do that, you're inviting wisdom and an acceleration of knowledge. You're inviting God's blessings.

Call Yourself Blessed

"Yet who knows whether you have come to the kingdom for such a time as this?"

ESTHER 4:14 NKJV

When I first started ministering back in 1999, I had *never* done this before, and I was very nervous. Negative thoughts bombarded my mind: *Joel, you're going to make a fool of yourself. Nobody is going to listen to you. Why should they?* I had to counter those thoughts by saying under my breath, "Joel, you are well able. You are equipped. You've been raised up for such a time as this." I didn't feel confident, but I called myself confident. I didn't feel anointed, but I called myself anointed.

You may not feel blessed, but you need to call yourself blessed. You may not feel healthy today, but don't go around telling everyone how you're not going to make it. Start calling yourself healthy, whole, strong, full of energy and full of life.

Silence Is Golden

"Do not shout; do not even talk," Joshua commanded. "Not a single word from any of you until I tell you to shout. Then shout!"

JOSHUA 6:10 NLT

When Joshua was leading the people of Israel into the Promised Land, they had to conquer the city of Jericho, which was surrounded by a huge, thick, tall wall made up of stone and mortar. They had no way to get in. But God told them to do something that sounded strange—for six days they were to march around that wall once a day, and on the seventh day they were to march around it seven times. If that wasn't odd enough, God gave them one final command: "While you're marching, keep totally silent."

God knew that after a couple of times around the perimeter of the walls, they would be saying, "This wall is never going to fall." Negative words would have kept them out of the Promised Land.

Just Keep Marching

There is...a time to be silent and a time to speak.

ECCLESIASTES 3:1, 7

God did not allow the Israelites to speak as they marched around Jericho. Why? He knew they would talk themselves out of it. In fact, it had happened years before. Their parents and their relatives were camped next door to the Promised Land, but shortly after the spies came back and told everyone how big their enemies were, all two million people were complaining, saying, "We don't have a chance. We'll never defeat these enemies" (see Numbers 13, 14). Even though they were right on the doorstep, their negative words kept them from going in.

There are times in all our lives where it's difficult to be positive. And that's okay. Just stay silent. Don't tell everyone what you're thinking. Keep marching in silence and the walls will come tumbling down.

The Walls Will Fall

But the people remained silent and said
nothing in reply, because the king had
commanded, "Do not answer him."

2 KINGS 18:36

Could it be that negative words are keeping you out of your promised land? Could it be that if you would not talk about how big the problem is, not complain about what didn't work out, not tell a friend how you're never going to break that addiction, maybe the walls that are holding you back would come down? Imagine behind that wall is your healing, your promotion, your dream coming to pass. Every day, so to speak, you're walking around the wall. What are you saying?

God is saying to us, "If you can't say anything positive and full of faith, don't say anything at all." Don't let your negative words keep you from God's best. If you'll stop talking defeat and simply remain silent, God can bring those walls down.

A Time of Testing

Do everything without grumbling or arguing, so that you may become blameless and pure, "children of God without fault in a warped and crooked generation."

PHILIPPIANS 2:14–15

FEBRUARY

11

When we're marching around the walls of our Jerichos, sometimes we go day after day and don't see anything happening. Just like them, the thoughts come swirling around our heads, *You didn't hear God right. Nothing is changing, and it's never going to happen.* No, that is a time of testing. You may have been doing it a year, two years, or five years. You thought it would have happened by now.

Pass that test. Don't start complaining. Don't do like the first group of Israelites that stopped at the door of the Promised Land and said, "Oh, what's the use? Let's just settle here." When the negative thoughts come, let them die stillborn. You will come into your seventh day. God is a faithful God. He will do what He has promised you.

All Is Well

And she answered,
"All is well."

2 KINGS 4:26 ESV

Second Kings 4 tells the remarkable story of a woman who was a good friend of the prophet Elisha. Her beloved young son is taken ill out in the field, carried home, where he dies in her arms. Devastated beyond measure, this heartbroken mother's story did not end here. Rather, she sets out immediately to enlist Elisha's help, but twice before she reaches him she is asked what is going on. Speaking words of faith, her only answer is, "All is well."

In her darkest hour, even in the midst of overwhelming tragedy, this lady refused to get negative and speak defeat. She chose to speak faith even though her mind was being bombarded with doubt. "All is well." That's when the most powerful force in the universe went to work, and her son's life was restored.

FEBRUARY
12

Speak Faith

...there was the boy lying dead on his couch.... Elisha... stretched out on him once more. The boy sneezed seven times and opened his eyes.

2 KINGS 4:32, 35

Continuing yesterday's story, Elisha went with the heartbroken mother, prayed for her son, and he miraculously came back to life. What I want you to see, however, is that despite all the negative thoughts that this woman was fighting, she still said, "All is well."

A lot of times when we face difficulties and somebody asks us how everything is going, we do just the opposite and tell them everything that's wrong. When you're hurting, you've been through a disappointment, and you've suffered a loss, you have to do what she did. Say it by faith, "All is well." It may not look well. It may not feel well. In the natural you should be complaining, talking about how bad it is, but instead you're making a declaration of faith.

All Things Are Possible

Then Moses stretched out his hand over the sea, and all that night the LORD drove the sea back with a strong east wind and turned it into dry land. The waters were divided.

EXODUS 14:21

God can resurrect dead dreams. He can resurrect a dead marriage. He can resurrect health that's going down or a business that's failing. When you get in agreement with God, all things are possible. You may be facing a big obstacle. It doesn't look good. But here's a key: Don't talk about the size of your problem. Talk about the size of your God. There was a day when God stopped the sun for Joshua. He parted the Red Sea for the Israelites. He breathed new life into the mother's little boy. He can turn your situation around as well. He can make a way even though you don't see a way.

My challenge today is: Don't let your negative words stop what God wants to do. Don't be snared by your words.

February 15

Your Promised Land

*"O our God...We do not know what to do,
but our eyes are on You."*

2 CHRONICLES 20:12 AMP

In the tough times—when you feel like
complaining, when you've got a good reason to be sour, because you lost a job, or a
friend did you wrong, or you're not feeling
well—you have to dig your heels in and say
it by faith, "This is difficult, but all is well.
God is still on the throne. He's the Lord my
Provider."

When you make this adjustment, God
is going to release promises that have been
delayed. What you've been praying about—
breaking that addiction, meeting the right
person, getting healthy again, starting that
business—suddenly, things are going to fall
into place. You're going to see God's favor
in a new way. He's going to break down
walls and bring you into your promised
land.

Say So

*Let the redeemed of the L*ORD *say so, whom
He has redeemed from the hand of the enemy...*

PSALM 107:2 NKJV

Words have creative power. When you speak something out, you give life to what you're saying. For instance, it's important to believe that you're blessed. But when you say, "I am blessed," that's when blessings come looking for you.

The Scripture says, "Let the redeemed of the Lord *say so*." It doesn't say, "Let the redeemed think so, or believe so, or hope so." That's all good, but you have to take it one step further and *say so*. If you're going to go to the next level, you have to *say so*. If you're going to accomplish a dream, overcome an obstacle, or break an addiction, you have to start declaring it. It has to come out of your mouth. That's how you give life to your faith.

When He Spoke

*And God said, "Let there be light,"
and there was light.*

GENESIS 1:3

When God created the worlds, He didn't just think them into being. He didn't just believe there would be light and land and oceans and animals. He had it in His heart, but nothing happened until He spoke. He said, "Let there be light," and light came. His thoughts didn't set it into motion; His words set it into motion.

It's the same principle today. You can have faith in your heart, big dreams, be standing on God's promises, and never see anything change. What's the problem? Nothing happens until you speak. Instead of just believing you're going to get out of debt, you have to say so. Declare every day, "I am coming out of debt. God's favor surrounds me like a shield." When you speak, good breaks, promotion, and ideas will track you down.

Activate Your Faith

*"With long life I will satisfy him
and show him my salvation."*

PSALM 91:16

When you get sick, instead of just thinking, *I hope I get over this illness. I'm praying I'll get better,* which is good, take it one more step and start declaring it. "I am strong. I am healthy. With long life God is going to satisfy me." That's what activates your faith.

It's not just hoping you have a good year or just hoping that you accomplish your dreams. Hope is good, but nothing happens until you speak. Before you leave the house every day, declare it: "This is going to be my best year. Things have shifted in my favor. I'm going to a new level." When you talk like that, the angels go to work, opening up new doors, lining up the right people, and arranging things in your favor.

"I Will Say"

I will say of the LORD, "He is my refuge and my fortress, my God, in whom I trust."

PSALM 91:2

The psalmist says, "I will say of the Lord," and in the next verse adds, "He will deliver and cover me." Notice the connection. *I will say* and *He will do*. It doesn't say, "I believe He is my refuge." The psalmist went around speaking it out: "The Lord is my refuge." Notice what happened. God became his refuge. God was saying in effect, "If you're bold enough to speak it, I'm bold enough to do it."

Have you ever declared that your dreams are coming to pass? Whatever God has put in your heart, talk about it like it's already on the way: "When I get married…, when I graduate from college…, when I see my family restored…" Not if it's going to happen, but when it's going to happen. That's your faith being released.

Do Not Give Up

*...those who seek the LORD
lack no good thing.*

PSALM 34:10

O ne of our staff members had been trying for over ten years to have a baby
with no success. Her doctors told her it
wasn't going to happen. One day she said,
"When I have my baby...," even though she
wasn't pregnant yet. She kept on speaking
about it for years. What was she doing? Saying so. She didn't just believe it. She was
declaring it. In the natural, it looked impossible. Most people would have given up, but
not this lady. She kept saying so: "When my
baby shows up..." Twenty years later, she
gave birth to twins.

She declared of the Lord and God did
what He promised. But think about the
opposite of Psalm 91:2: "I will not say of the
Lord, and He will not do." That's the principle.

All Your Needs

And my God will meet all your needs according to the riches of his glory in Christ Jesus.

PHILIPPIANS 4:19

When we were trying to acquire the Compaq Center to become our church building, Victoria and I would drive around it and say, "That's our building. Father, thank You that You are making a way where we don't see a way." We prayed about it, believed that it would happen, and then we took the most important step and declared that it was ours. It became a part of our everyday conversation. "When we renovate it..." "When we have the grand opening..."

We didn't say, "I don't know. Where are we going to get the funds?" No, we said of the Lord, as the psalmist did, "God, we know You are bigger than any obstacle. We know You are supplying all our needs." We declared it, and God did it.

FEBRUARY 22

Declare Victory

Their children will be mighty in the land;
the generation of the upright will be blessed.

PSALM 112:2

What are you saying of the Lord? Are you declaring victory over your life, family, and career? Nothing happens until you speak. When you get up in the morning, make some declarations of faith. I declare every day, "My children will fulfill their destinies. Their gifts and talents will come out to the full."

Whatever God has put in your heart, declare that it will come to pass. You have to speak favor into your future. Don't talk about how big your problem is. Talk about how big your God is. When you say of the Lord, "You're my healer, my way maker, my dream giver, my restorer, my vindicator, my health, my peace, my victory," that's when God will show up and do more than you can ask or think.

Speak Favor

*By Your favor and grace,
O LORD, you have made my
mountain stand strong...*

PSALM 30:7 AMP

FEBRUARY

23

Ever since I took over for my father in the church, I have said, "When people turn me on, on television, they cannot turn me off." Do you know how many letters I get from people who say, "Joel, I was flipping through the channels. I don't like TV preachers. I never watch TV preachers, but when I turned you on, I couldn't turn you off"? I think to myself, *I called you in! I said so.*

When you declare favor over your life and over your future, God will make things happen that should have never happened. Our attitude should be, *I'm coming out of debt, and I'm saying so. I will overcome every obstacle, and I'm saying so. I will accomplish my dreams, and I'm saying so.*

"I Shall Be"

FEBRUARY

24

When she heard about Jesus,
she came behind Him in
the crowd and touched His
garment. For she said,
"If only I may touch His
clothes, I shall be made well."

MARK 5:27–28 NKJV

This lady had been sick for many years and spent all her money trying to get well, but nothing worked. When she heard Jesus was coming through town, she kept saying to herself, "I shall be made well." She wasn't saying, "It's no use." No, she kept saying to herself, "When I get to Jesus, I shall be made whole." She was prophesying victory. All through the day, she kept saying, "Healing is on its way. Brighter days are up ahead."

When she started making her way through the thick crowd to Jesus, she didn't complain but just kept saying, "This is my time. Things are changing in my favor." The more she said it, the closer she got. Finally she reached out and touched the edge of His robe and she was instantly healed.

Move toward Jesus

Throwing his cloak aside, [the blind man] jumped to his feet and came to Jesus.

MARK 10:50

From yesterday's reading, notice the principle: As the sick lady kept saying she would be made well, she kept moving in the direction of Jesus. Whatever you're constantly saying, you're moving toward. You may be struggling in your finances, but every time you declare, "I am blessed. I am prosperous. I have the favor of God," you're moving toward increase. You're getting closer to seeing that come to pass.

You may be facing a sickness. It doesn't look good. But every time you declare, "I am healthy. I am strong. I am getting better," you're moving toward health, wholeness, victory. Perhaps you're struggling with an addiction. Every time you declare, "I am free. This addiction does not control me," you're moving toward freedom. You're moving toward breakthroughs.

Use Your Words

God, who gives life to the dead and calls those things which do not exist as though they did...

ROMANS 4:17 NKJV

We have seen that whatever you're constantly saying, you're moving toward. If you're always saying, "I've been through so much. I'll never be happy again," you're moving toward more discouragement, more sadness. If you will change what you're saying, you will change what you're seeing. The Scripture says, "Call those things which do not exist as though they did."

A lot of times we do just the opposite. We call the things that are as if they will always be that way. "Taxes are so high. I don't see how I'm going to make it." You're calling in more struggle, more lack. "I can't stand my job." You're calling in more frustration, more defeat. Don't use your words to describe the situation. Use your words to change the situation.

Be Renewed

Although Moses was a hundred and twenty years old when he died, his eyesight was not dim, nor his natural strength abated.

DEUTERONOMY 34:7 AMP

A gentleman who looked to be about seventy told me, "Joel, when you get old, it's all downhill." That was his declaring, "I'm going down." He was calling in poor health, lack of vision, and loss of hearing. By the way he looked, he had already been saying it for a long time!

I realize we're all going to get old, but don't make plans to go downhill. Consider Moses at one hundred and twenty years old. Healthy. Strong. 20/20 vision. Sharp mind. In spite of how you may feel, every day you need to declare, "My youth is being renewed. Like Moses, I will finish my course with my eye not dim, my natural strength not abated." You talk like that, and you're moving toward renewed youth, health, energy, and vitality.

Become What You Believe

He touched their eyes and said, "Become what you believe." It happened. They saw.

MATTHEW 9:29 MSG

There's a young lady on staff at Lakewood. Every morning before she leaves her house, she looks in the mirror and says, "Girl, you're looking good today." I saw her one time and asked if she was still doing it. She said, "Yeah, in fact, today when I looked in the mirror, I said, 'Girl, some days you look good; but today, you look *really* good.'"

Have a better *say so*. Don't talk about the way you are. Talk about the way you want to be. Stop talking about all the things you don't like—how you're getting too old, too wrinkled, too this, too that. Start calling yourself strong, healthy, talented, beautiful, and young. Every morning, before you leave your house, look in the mirror and say, "Good morning, you good-looking thing!"

Move Forward

"Be strong and courageous. Do not fear or be dismayed because...the One with us is greater than the one with him."

2 CHRONICLES 32:7 AMP

Maybe you're in a difficult time today. To complain, "I don't think I'll ever get out," is just going to draw in more defeat. Your declaration should be, "I have grace for this season. Those who are for me are greater than those who are against me." When you say that, strength comes. Courage comes. Confidence comes. Endurance comes.

If you go through a disappointment, a bad break, or a loss, don't grumble, "I don't know why this has happened to me. It's so unfair." That's just going to draw in more self-pity. Your declaration should be, "God promised me beauty for ashes, joy for mourning. I'm moving forward. New beginnings are in my future." You talk like that, and you're moving away from self-pity and toward God's goodness in a new way.

Every Morning

*You have crowned him
with glory and honor.*

PSALM 8:5 NKJV

One of the best things we can do is take a few minutes every morning and make positive declarations over our lives. Write down not only your dreams, your goals, and your vision, but make a list of any area you want to improve in, anything you want to see changed. Put that list on your bathroom mirror, somewhere private. Before you leave the house, take a couple of minutes and declare that over your life.

If you struggle with your self-esteem, feeling less than, you need to declare every day, "I am confident. I am valuable. I am one of a kind. I am wearing a crown of honor. I am a child of the Most High God." You declare that, and you'll go out with your shoulders back, with your head held high.

"I Am Strong!"

*Let the weak say,
"I am strong!"*

JOEL 3:10 AMP

The Scripture doesn't say, "Let the weak talk about the weakness. Discuss the weakness. Call five friends and explain the weakness." You have to send your words out in the direction you want your life to go.

When you're in a tough time and somebody asks you how you're doing, don't go through a sad song of everything that's wrong in your life. "Oh, man, my back's been hurting. Traffic is so bad today. My boss isn't treating me right. The dishwasher broke. The goldfish died, and my dog doesn't like me." All that's going to do is draw in more defeat. Turn it around. Have a report of victory. "I am blessed. I am healthy. I am prosperous. I have the favor of God." What you consistently talk about, you're moving toward.

Your Destiny Awaits

"You come to me with a sword, with a spear, and with a javelin. But I come to you in the name of the LORD of hosts... whom you have defied."

1 SAMUEL 17:45 NKJV

When David faced Goliath, it looked impossible. He could have easily gone around saying, "Look at him. He's twice my size. He's got more experience, more equipment, more talent. This is never going to work out." You can talk yourself out of your destiny. Negative words can keep you from becoming who you were created to be.

David looked Goliath in the eyes and said, "This day I will defeat you and feed your head to the birds of the air!" He prophesied victory. He may have felt fear, but he spoke faith. I can hear David, affirming under his breath, "I am well able. I am anointed. If God be for me, who dare be against me?" He picked up that rock, slung it in his slingshot, and Goliath came tumbling down.

Our Father

*"But as for me and my household,
we will serve the LORD."*

JOSHUA 24:15

When you face giants in life, you have to do as David did and prophesy your future. "Cancer, you are no match for me. I will defeat you." "This addiction may have been in my family for years, but this is a new day. I'm the difference maker. I am free." "My child may have been off course for a long time, but I know it's only temporary. As for me and my house, we will serve the Lord."

Say to that loneliness, that addiction, that legal problem, "Don't you know who I am? A child of the Most High God. My Father created the universe. He breathed life into me and crowned me with His favor. He called me more than a conqueror. That means you can't defeat me. You can't hold me back."

Talk to the Mountain

"So, big mountain, who do you think you are? Next to Zerubbabel you're nothing but a molehill."

ZECHARIAH 4:7 MSG

Zerubbabel faced a huge mountain. To rebuild the temple in Jerusalem was a big obstacle with enemies opposing every step. But he didn't talk about how impossible it was, how it was never going to work out. He said, "Mountain, you're nothing but a molehill." He was prophesying his future. The mountain looked big. But he declared it would be flattened out. It would become a molehill.

Here's the principle: Don't talk about the mountain; talk to the mountain. Look at that mountain of debt and tell it, "You can't defeat me. I will lend and not borrow." Whatever mountains you face in life, no matter how big they look, don't shrink back in fear or be intimidated. Prophesy victory. Prophesy breakthroughs. Prophesy what you're believing for.

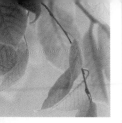

Come Alive

"Prophesy to these bones and say to them, 'Dry bones, hear the word of the LORD!... I will make breath enter you, and you will come to life.'"

EZEKIEL 37:4–5

Ezekiel saw a vision of a valley filled with bones. It was like a huge graveyard of bones from people who had died. Bones represent things in our life that look dead, situations that seem impossible and permanently unchanging. God told him to do something interesting. He said, "Ezekiel, prophesy to these dead bones." Ezekiel started speaking to the bones, telling them to come back to life. As he was speaking, the bones started rattling and coming together, morphing back into people. Finally, breath came into those bodies, and they stood up like "a vast army."

You may have things in your life that seem dead—a relationship, a business, your health. It's not enough to just pray about it; you need to speak to it. Prophesy to those dead bones as Ezekiel did.

New Life

*"Prophesy to the breath;
prophesy, son of man,
and say to it,...'Come,
breath, from the four winds
and breathe into these slain,
that they may live.'"*

EZEKIEL 37:9

Perhaps like Ezekiel, all you can see is a valley of dry bones, so to speak. Call in health. Call in abundance. Call in restoration. That child who's been off course, don't just pray about him or her. Prophesy and say, "Son, daughter, come back in. You will fulfill your destiny." Get your checkbook out and prophesy to it. All it looks like are dead bones. Debt. Lack. Struggle. "I prophesy to these dead bones that I will lend and not borrow. I am the head and not the tail. I am coming into overflow."

Just as with Ezekiel, if you'll prophesy to the bones, God will resurrect what looks dead. He'll make things happen that you could never make happen.

Day After Day

*...the tongue of
the wise brings healing.*

PROVERBS 12:18

A friend of mine had tried to stop smoking cigarettes again and again but couldn't. For years she said, "I can't do it. But if I do, I'll gain so much weight." One day someone told her to start saying, "I don't like to smoke. I'm going to quit and not gain weight," even while she was smoking and enjoying it. Day after day, she prophesied victory. She wasn't talking about the way she was. She was talking about the way she wanted to be.

Three months later, she noticed the cigarettes tasted almost bitter. It got worse and worse. Several months later, she couldn't stand it anymore. She stopped smoking, and she never gained one extra pound. She broke that addiction, in part, by the power of her words. She prophesied her future.

The Future Is Bright

"You intended to harm me, but God intended it all for good. He brought me to this position so I could save the lives of many people."

GENESIS 50:20 NLT

Maybe you've spent years saying negative things over your life. Let me lead you in a few "Say So"s. Make these declarations out loud.

"I will accomplish my dreams. The right people are in my future. The right opportunities are headed my way."

"I am the head and not the tail. I will lend and not borrow."

"I will overcome every obstacle. What was meant for my harm, God is using for my advantage. My future is bright."

"I run with purpose in every step. I will have everything God intended for me to have. I am the redeemed of the Lord, and I *say so* today!"

The Commanded Blessing

"...if you diligently listen to and obey the voice of the LORD your God... All these blessings will come upon you and overtake you..."

DEUTERONOMY 28:1–2 AMP

When you honor God with your life, keeping Him in first place, He puts something on you called *a commanded blessing*. The commanded blessing is like a magnet. It attracts the right people, good breaks, contracts, ideas, resources, and influence. You don't have to go after these things, trying to make something happen in your own strength, your own talent; hoping that life works out. All you have to do is keep honoring God and the right people will find you. The right opportunities will come across your path. The favor, the wisdom, and the vindication will track you down.

Why? You've become a magnet for God's goodness.

March 11

Attract Goodness

*Every good and perfect gift is from above,
coming down from the Father of the heavenly lights,
who does not change like shifting shadows.*

JAMES 1:17

The military has what's called a heat-seeking missile that follows its target everywhere it goes and eventually overtakes it and accomplishes its purpose. In the same way, when you keep God in first place, He will send blessings that chase you down, favor that overtakes you. Out of nowhere, a good break comes. Suddenly, your health improves. Out of the blue, you're able to pay your house off. Unexpectedly, a dream comes to pass. That's not a coincidence. That's the commanded blessing on your life.

That means because you are honoring God, right now, something is attracted to you. Not fear, sickness, depression, or bad breaks. No, favor is tracking you down, promotion is headed your way, divine connections are searching you out. You are attracting the goodness of God.

A New Attitude

*"Then your light will break
forth like the dawn, and your
healing will quickly appear..."*

ISAIAH 58:8

Because you have a commanded blessing on your life, you have to start thinking that way. If you are facing an illness, instead of thinking, *I'm never going to get well. You should see the medical report,* your attitude should be, *Healing is looking for me. Restoration is tracking me down.* If you're struggling in your finances, instead of thinking, *I'll never get out of debt. I'll never accomplish my dreams,* you need to tell yourself, *Abundance is looking for me. Favor is in my future. Good breaks are tracking me down.* If you're single, don't conclude, *I'll never get married. I'm too old. It's been too long.* No, your thoughts need to declare, *The right person is looking for me. Divine connections are tracking me down. They're already in my future. Like a magnet, I'm drawing them in.*

Exceedingly
Abundantly

*Now to Him who is able to do
exceedingly abundantly above
all that we ask or think, according
to the power that works in us...*

EPHESIANS 3:20 NKJV

When I look back over my life, it is
evident that most of the favor and
good breaks came to me. I didn't go after
them. I was simply being my best, and God
did more than I could ask or think. I never
thought I could stand up in front of people
and minister. I spent seventeen years
behind the scenes at Lakewood faithfully
doing the television production. I gave it my
all. I'd went the extra mile to make sure that
every broadcast was as perfect as possible.

I wasn't looking to become Lakewood's
senior pastor. I was content where I was
behind the scenes. But when my father
went to be with the Lord, this opportunity
came looking for me. I never planned on
doing it; it chased me down.

Like a Magnet

*"What no eye has seen, what
no ear has heard, and what no
human mind has conceived"—
the things God has prepared
for those who love him...*

1 CORINTHIANS 2:9

When I was in my early twenties, I
walked into a jewelry store and met
Victoria for the first time. We went out on
our first date and had so much fun. The
next week she invited me to dinner and
we had a great time. That was followed by
repeated calls from me to her, but she was
always either busy or not available. Finally,
I assumed she didn't want to see me, and I
stopped calling. About two weeks later, she
saw me in a small diner and said, "Joel, I'm
so sorry I keep missing your calls."

God's dream for our lives is so much
bigger than our own. When you honor God,
you won't have to go after it; it will come to
you. Like a magnet, you'll draw it in.

Be Your Best

The LORD bestows grace and favor and honor; no good thing will He withhold from those who walk uprightly.

PSALM 84:11 AMP

God has the right people in your future. When you honor God, the person He has designed for you, the right one, will come across your path as though drawn by a magnet. He'll cause you to be at the right place at the right time. You don't have to play games and try to convince somebody to like you. If they don't celebrate you and see you as a gift, a treasure, as one of a kind, move forward. The one whom God designed for you will think you're the greatest thing in the world.

If you will keep being your best right where you are, honoring God, you will come into favor, promotion, and opportunity bigger than you ever imagined.

Be Steadfast

Jotham grew powerful because he walked steadfastly before the LORD his God.

2 CHRONICLES 27:6

If God were to show you right now what He has planned for you and where He's taking you—the favor, the promotion, the influence—it would boggle your mind. It's not going to happen just because of your talent, your personality, or your hard work. It's going to happen because of the commanded blessing on your life. God's anointing on you is more important than your talent, your education, or what family you come from. You could have less talent, but with the favor of God, you will go further than people who have much more talent.

If you'll just keep getting to work on time, doing more than you have to, being a person of excellence and integrity, the right people will find you and the right opportunities will track you down.

Pass the Tests

"His master replied, 'Well done, good and faithful servant! You have been faithful with a few things; I will put you in charge of many things. Come and share your master's happiness!'"

MATTHEW 25:21

Don't be frustrated if God's plans for your life don't happen on your time-table. You have to pass some tests. You have to prove to God that you'll be faithful right where you are. If you're not faithful in the wilderness, how can God trust you to be faithful in the promised land? You have to keep a good attitude when you're not getting your way. You have to be your best when you're not getting any credit. Do the right thing when it's difficult. That's when your character is being developed.

If you will pass these tests, you can be certain God will get you to where you're supposed to be. The right people are in your future. So are the right opportunities, the good breaks, the wisdom, the contracts, the houses.

Explosive Blessings

You need to persevere so that when you have done the will of God, you will receive what he has promised.

HEBREWS 10:36

I've learned that in a split second one touch of God's favor can take you further than you could go in your whole lifetime on your own. Quit thinking, *I'm getting further behind. I'll never accomplish my dreams.* No, God has explosive blessings in your future. He has blessings that will thrust you years and years ahead.

You say, "This sounds good, but I don't really have the talent. I don't know the right people. I don't have the money." That's okay; God does. He's already lined up everything you need. There are good breaks right now that have your name on them. If you'll keep honoring God, being your best, like a magnet, you're going to draw in what already has your name on it.

Your Name Is on It

"But for you who fear my name, the Sun of Righteousness will rise with healing in his wings."

MALACHI 4:2 NLT

Perhaps you've been waiting for God to provide for a need in your life and you're asking when it's going to happen. It will happen at the exact right time. Don't get discouraged. God knows what He's doing. If it had happened earlier, it wouldn't have been the best time. Just keep being faithful right where you are and keep living with an attitude that something good is coming your way.

When you do that, you're going to draw in like a magnet what already has your name on it. There's healing with your name on it. If you're single, there's a spouse with your name on him or her. There's a business with your name on it. God has already chosen what you need to be yours.

Eventually

...the wealth of the sinner [finds its way eventually] into the hands of the righteous, for whom it was laid up.

PROVERBS 13:22 AMPC

You don't have to seek the blessings of God. Seek God, and the blessings will seek after you. This is where we miss it. Very often, we think, *I have to get this promotion. I have to meet this person. I must get my career going faster.* And yes, we have to use our talent, be determined, and take steps of faith. But you can stay in peace. You can live at rest, knowing that because you're honoring God, the right people and the right opportunities will find you.

Notice, because you're the righteous, there's something God has laid up for you. The good news is, at the right time, "eventually" it's going to find you. Keep honoring God, and He promises some of these "eventually"s are going to track you down.

Seek First His Kingdom

MARCH

21

"But seek first his kingdom and his righteousness, and all these things will be given to you as well."

MATTHEW 6:33

In yesterday's reading I mentioned there are some "eventually"s in your future. Our beautiful facility, the former Compaq Center, is an "eventually." It was laid up for us. It had our name on it, and at the right time, it found us. The building was first called the Summit, but I believe if you would have peeled back the name when it was built in the early 1970s, you would have seen the name, "Lakewood Church." God had us in mind when they built it. Eventually, God said, "All right, it's time to hand it over."

The great thing is that you don't have to go after "eventually"s; just go after God. Keep Him in first place. Live a life of excellence and integrity, and God promises the "eventually"s will find their way into your hands.

Ask, Seek, Knock

"Ask and it will be given to you; seek and you will find;
knock and the door will be opened to you."

MATTHEW 7:7

I said that our church facility is one of
God's "eventually"s for us. The amazing
thing is that I didn't go after it; it came to
me. Twice, I tried to buy land and build a
new sanctuary, but both times, the property was sold out from under us. I thought,
We're stuck. There's no way to grow. But
when I got the unexpected news that the
Compaq Center was for sale, something
came alive on the inside of me. I never
dreamed we could have a premier facility in
the fourth largest city in America, and it's
on the second busiest freeway in the nation.

As was true for us, the "eventually"s
God has lined up for you are going to boggle
your mind. It's going to be more than you
can ask or think.

Pleasing God

Our purpose is to please God, not people.
He alone examines the motives of our hearts.

1 THESSALONIANS 2:4 NLT

Jesus said that everything you need to fulfill your destiny has already been laid up for you. Now you just have to make pleasing God your highest priority. In other words, when temptation comes, be firm and say, "No, thanks. I'm going to please God. I want to fulfill my destiny. I want to come in to my 'eventually's." Before you tell that person off, stop and declare, "No, I'm going to please God and keep my mouth closed." At the office, when they're not treating you right and you feel like slacking off, overcome that attitude and state, "I'm going to please God and keep being my best. I know I'm not working unto people; I'm working unto God."

You live like that, and all the forces of darkness cannot keep you from your destiny.

A Servant of Christ

*Am I now trying to win the approval
of human beings, or of God?
Or am I trying to please people? If
I were still trying to please people, I
would not be a servant of Christ.*

GALATIANS 1:10

God has not only already arranged for
the "eventually"s in your life; He's
taken it one step further. He's already put
your name on them. They've already been
marked as a part of your divine destiny. You
may not have seen it yet, but don't get discouraged.

What's your part? Worry? Struggle? Try
to make it happen? Manipulate this person,
and maybe they'll do you a favor? No, you
don't have to play up to people. You don't
have to beg people, hope that they'll throw
you a crumb here or there. You are not a
beggar; you are a child of the Most High
God. You have royal blood flowing through
your veins. You are wearing a crown of
favor. The Creator of the universe has called
you, equipped you, empowered you, and
chosen you.

Honoring God

*"But now the Lord declares:
'Far be it from me!
Those who honor me I will honor..."*

1 SAMUEL 2:30

Right now, something's looking for you—not defeat, struggle, lack. You are the righteous. Favor is looking for you. Good breaks are looking for you. Healing is looking for you. Influence is looking for you.

The right people will show up, the ones who want to help you. The good breaks, the businesses, and the contracts will track you down. One phone call, one person whom God has ordained to help you, can change the course of your life. How is this going to happen? Is it just through your talent, your ability, and your hard work? That's part of it, but the main key is by honoring God. That's what puts you in a position for His blessings to overtake you. That's what makes you a magnet for His favor.

First Have Hope

"The LORD your God will make you abundantly prosperous in all the work of your hand..."

DEUTERONOMY 30:9 ESV

You are a powerful magnet. You may be very close to attracting that for which you've been praying and believing. You've honored God. You've been faithful. Now God is about to release an "eventually" in your life. It's going to be bigger than you imagined. When you receive it, it's going to be better for you than you ever dreamed. You're going to say, "It was well worth the wait."

"Well, you're just getting my hopes up." You're right. You can't have faith if you don't first have hope. It's easy to get stuck in a rut, thinking, *God has been good to me. I have a good family. I'm healthy. I'm blessed.* But you haven't seen anything yet. You haven't scratched the surface of what God has in store.

Open Doors

"Behold, I have set before you an open door, which no one is able to shut."

REVELATION 3:8 ESV

If you had told me years ago that one day I would be ministering around the world and have books translated into different languages, I would have thought, *Not me. I don't have anything to say.* But God knows what He's put in you—the gifts, the talents, the potential. You have seeds of greatness on the inside. Doors are going to open that no man can shut. Talent is going to come out of you that you didn't know you had. God is going to connect you with the right people. He will present you with opportunities that will thrust you into a new level of your destiny.

Dream big. Believe big. Pray big. Make room for God to do something new in your life.

Rewards

Trouble chases sinners,
while blessings reward the righteous.

PROVERBS 13:21 NLT

You have become the righteousness of God in Christ Jesus. Right now, you are being rewarded with the favor of God. Promotion is chasing you. Healing is chasing you. Victory is coming your way. Good ideas will come to you that will touch people's lives. You might start a ministry in your church or a business that is like nothing you've ever thought about. God has raised you up to take new ground for the kingdom, to go where others have not gone.

You don't have to worry about how it's all going to work out. God knows how to have the blessings find you. What has your name on it—the real estate, the good breaks, the businesses, the favor—will eventually find its way into your hands.

Guard Your Heart

Above all else, guard your heart,
for everything you do flows from it.

PROVERBS 4:23

Don't ever say, "I'll never get out of debt." "I'll never get married." "I'll never be well again." Do you know what that's doing? Demagnetizing your magnet. It's taking away the attraction power that God has put in you—the gifts, the talents, the potential.

When I was a little boy, I used to play with a magnet. One day I discovered the magnet had lost its drawing power. I had left it by something that demagnetized it. It looked the same, but it wouldn't attract anything. In the same way, when we dwell on negative thoughts—*can't do it, not able to, never going to happen*—that is demagnetizing our magnet. You are taking away its power to pull in what belongs to you.

Make Room for More

"Enlarge your house; build an addition. Spread out your home, and spare no expense! For you will soon be bursting at the seams."

ISAIAH 54:2–3 NLT

Each of us can look back over our life and remember a time when we unexpectedly saw God's favor. You didn't go after it; it came after you. God has done it in the past, and the good news is He's not only going to do it again in the future, but what He's going to show you will make what you've seen pale in comparison. He has explosive blessings coming your way. You're going to look back and join me in saying, "How in the world did I get here? I'm not the most qualified or the most talented. I don't have all the experience." You may not, but God does. He knows how to get you to where you're supposed to be. All through the day, make this declaration: "I am blessed."

Something Good

"I will give you hidden treasures, riches stored in secret places, so that you may know that I am the LORD, the God of Israel, who summons you by name."

ISAIAH 45:3

When you realize God has put a commanded blessing on your life, and you go out each day with the attitude that something good is going to happen to you, that's when God can do the exceedingly abundantly above and beyond.

I believe you're about to draw in good breaks, promotion, healing, favor, ideas, contracts, and creativity. God is about to release what already has your name on it. You're not going to have to go after it; it's going to come after you. It's going to be bigger than you imagined. It's going to happen sooner than you thought. You're about to step into the fullness of your destiny and become everything God has created you to be.

Be Transformed

Do not conform to the pattern of this world, but be transformed by the renewing of your mind. Then you will be able to test and approve what God's will is—his good, pleasing and perfect will.

ROMANS 12:2

When we've struggled in an area for a long time, it's easy to think, *This is the way it's always going to be. I'll always struggle in my finances. My marriage will never improve.* Too often we see it as permanent. People tell me, "I've always been negative. That's just who I am." They've convinced themselves that it's never going to change.

The first place we lose the battle is in our own thinking. If you think it's permanent, then it's permanent. If you think you've reached your limits, you have. If you think you'll never get well, you won't. You have to change your thinking. You need to see everything that's holding you back— every limitation, every addiction, every sickness—as only temporary. It didn't come to stay; it came to pass.

Don't Settle

...the people of Judah were victorious because they relied on the LORD, the God of their ancestors.

2 CHRONICLES 13:18

You may have struggled in an area for years. The medical report says, "Just learn to live with it." But there is another report. It says, "God is restoring health back to you. The number of your days He will fulfill." Your attitude should be, *This sickness is on foreign territory. I am a temple of the Most High God.* In your career you may feel stuck. You haven't had a good break in a long time. You've gone as far as your education allows. It's easy to think, *I've reached my limits.* All through the day you should declare, "I'm not settling here. My greatest victories are still out in front of me."

If you will just break out in your thinking, you will see things begin to improve.

Break Strongholds

*The weapons we fight with are not the weapons
of the world. On the contrary, they have divine
power to demolish strongholds.*

2 CORINTHIANS 10:4

The moment you accept that something
negative is the norm, the moment you
decide, *This is my lot in life,* that's when
it can take root and become a reality. A
stronghold in your mind is formed that can
keep you from your destiny.

You have to stir up your faith. God is
not limited by your education, by your
nationality, or by your background. But He
is limited by your thinking. I'm asking you
to stand against the lies of permanency, lies
that state, "You'll never lose that weight.
You'll never break that addiction. You'll
never own your own house." When those
thoughts come, dismiss them. Don't give
them the time of day. God is saying, "It's
not permanent; it's temporary. It didn't
come to stay; it came to pass."

Set Free

*If any of your people—Hebrew men or women—
sell themselves to you and serve you six years,
in the seventh year you must let them go free.*

DEUTERONOMY 15:12

God gave His people this law that said every seventh year they had to release any Hebrew slaves. If you were Hebrew and owed someone money that you couldn't pay, they could take you in as a slave and make you work until you paid them back. But every seventh year, no matter how in debt you were, God's people were set free. All the pain, struggling, and suffering was gone in one day.

This tells me God never intended His people to be a permanent slave to anything. You may be in debt today, but God did not intend that to last forever. You may be facing an illness, but it is only temporary. You may be struggling with an addiction, but it's not going to keep you in bondage.

Your Seventh Year

"So if the Son sets you free,
you will be free indeed."

JOHN 8:36

As was true for the Hebrew slaves, the seventh year is when you break free from limitations that are holding you back—sickness, addictions, debt, constant struggles. It looked as though it would never change, but then one touch of God's favor and it suddenly turns around. Suddenly you get a good break. Suddenly your health improves. Suddenly a dream comes to pass. What happened? You came into a seventh year.

Quit telling yourself, "This problem is permanent." You are a child of the Most High God. You are not going to be a permanent slave to anything. Get in agreement with God and affirm, "I'm coming into my seventh year. It is my time to break free. Every chain has been loosed. Every stronghold has come down. I know I have been released into increase."

It Is Possible

*But He said, "The things
which are impossible with
men are possible with God."*

LUKE 18:27 NKJV

For three years a man went through chemotherapy and radiation on a large tumor in his stomach area but nothing affected it. After two more years of no treatment and no change, he had one of our volunteer Prayer Partners pray over him. When he went back for more tests, the tumor had shrunk in half. The doctor didn't understand it, but the man mentioned the prayer. The doctor said, "Tell those people to keep praying, because at this pace it'll be totally gone in a few months!"

What was that? A seventh year. God is not limited to the natural. It doesn't matter how long it's been that way or how impossible it looks. When you come into your seventh year, all the forces of darkness cannot stop what God wants to do.

Released into Increase

"According to your faith let it be done to you."

MATTHEW 9:29

Are there limitations in your life you think are permanent? God is saying, "Get ready. You are coming into your seventh year." The seventh year is a year of release from sickness, chronic pain, depression, worry, and anxiety. Release from bad habits, from addictions. It's also a release into increase. God is about to release you into new opportunities, good breaks, and new levels. He is going to release ideas, creativity, sales, contracts, and business. The seventh year is when you get released into overflow. It's when dreams come to pass.

Now you have to receive this into your spirit today. This is for people who know things have shifted in their favor. It is for people who know every limitation is only temporary, for people who know they're entering into their seventh year.

The Favorable Year

"The Spirit of the Lord is upon Me...to proclaim the favorable year of the Lord [the day when salvation and the favor of God abound greatly]."

LUKE 4:18–19 AMP

In 2003, Lakewood signed a sixty-year lease with the City of Houston for our facility, the former Compaq Center. We wanted to own the facility, but the lease was the best thing at the time. Seven years later, in 2010, the city decided to sell some of their properties. They asked if we were interested in purchasing the facility, and of course we were, but it depended on the price. Brand new, a facility such as this would cost 400 million dollars. The city ran its own independent appraisal and said, "We'll sell it to you for seven and a half million dollars." Now we no longer lease. We own the property.

Isn't this interesting? Our seventh year for that price! Only God can do that. Friend, there are some seventh years in your future!

Get Ready

*"I will make rivers flow on barren heights,
and springs within the valleys. I will turn
the desert into pools of water, and the
parched ground into springs."*

ISAIAH 41:18

You may think, *I could never afford that house and property...never get well...never meet the right person.* No, you need to get ready. When you come into your seventh year, God is going to do more than you can ask or think. He is going to exceed your expectations. It's going to be bigger, better, and more rewarding than you thought possible. God is going to release you from leasing into owning. He'll release you from debt into abundance, from sickness into health, from constantly struggling into an anointing of ease.

Dare to say, "God, I want to thank You that I'm coming into my seventh year. Thank You that You are releasing me into the fullness of my destiny. I am free!" When you believe, all things are possible.

No Vacancy Here

*"Arise, shine, for your light has come,
and the glory of the LORD rises upon you."*

ISAIAH 60:1

Maybe you've lived with a sickness or chronic pain long enough. You've put up with that depression long enough. You've struggled with the addiction long enough. Hope has begun to fill your heart. God is saying, "This is your time. Get ready for release. Get ready for a breakthrough. Get ready for increase. Get ready for your seventh year."

How do you get ready? Stop taking ownership of those things. That sickness...that chronic pain...that financial difficulty is not a part of who you are. It may be there temporarily, but that's not where it's staying. In your mind, don't let it move in and take up residency. You need to have one of those signs out that says, "No Vacancy Here." Start thinking, start talking, and start acting as if it's going to change.

See It as Temporary

For our light affliction,
which is but for a moment,
is working for us a far
more exceeding and
eternal weight of glory.

APRIL

11

2 CORINTHIANS 4:17 NKJV

Your limitations may seem big, but by faith you need to see them as being light and temporary. This is what Moses did. The Israelites had been in slavery for hundreds of years. Moses had a son, whom he named Gershom, which means, "I am an alien in a strange land." Moses was making this declaration of faith: "We're in slavery, but slavery is not our norm. We are foreigners in this land. We won't be staying much longer."

When you confront a limitation, tell yourself, "I won't be staying here long. I am not a citizen. It may be where I am, but it is not who I am. I am blessed. I am healthy. I am strong. I am victorious." Anything to the contrary you need to see as foreign, as temporary.

Have a Boldness

*"This is what the LORD says:
Put your house in order,
because you are going to die."*

ISAIAH 38:1

King Hezekiah was very sick when the prophet who spoke for God announced he was going to die. Hezekiah could have accepted it and thought, *It's my lot in life.* But Hezekiah had a boldness. He chose to believe even when it looked impossible. The Scripture says, "He turned his face to the wall and started praying."

"God, I'm asking You to give me more years. God, I'm not finished. I've served You. My family has honored You. God, let me live longer." Before the prophet could leave the palace grounds, God spoke to him and said, "Go back and tell Hezekiah that I'm going to give him fifteen more years." Here's what I want you to see. Hezekiah's faith is what brought about his seventh year. Your faith is what causes God to move.

Believe It

The LORD will save me and we will sing with stringed instruments all the days of our lives in the temple of the LORD.

ISAIAH 38:20

As a follow up to yesterday's reading, what's interesting is that when Hezekiah got the news that God had said his life would be extended, he didn't feel any better. Here's the key: Hezekiah didn't wait for his health to turn around before he gave God praise and started talking as though he was going to live. It's easy to think, *When I see it, I'll believe it.* But faith says, "You have to believe it, and then you'll see it."

Like Isaiah, I've announced to you that you're coming into your seventh year. Look at your circumstances and say, "It doesn't look any different, but God, I believe I'm stepping into a new season of favor, that every limitation has been broken. I just want to thank You for Your goodness in my life."

It Only Looks Permanent

Enter his gates with thanksgiving and his courts with praise; give thanks to him and praise his name.

PSALM 100:4

We saw in Hezekiah's healing that our praise is what activates God's favor. When you have the boldness to talk as though it's going to happen, act as though it's going to happen, and praise as though it's going to happen, that's when God says to the angels, "Turn around and go back and tell them I'm going to change what looked permanent."

Are you releasing your faith? Are you thanking God that it's turning around? Are you declaring, "Where I am is not where I'm staying? This sickness is temporary. I'm coming out of debt. There are new levels in my future. I am free." When you have this attitude of faith, speaking victory over your life, that's when the Creator of the universe can show up and do amazing things.

April 15

Give Him Praise

Let the high praises of God be in their mouth...

PSALM 149:6 NKJV

A lot of times instead of taking our praise to God, we're taking our problems to Him. It's easy to turn prayer into a complaining session, but remember, God already knows your needs. You don't have to tell God everything that's wrong, what you don't like, and how long it's been that way.

It's much better to take your praise to God rather than your problems. Your financial situation may not look good, but turn it around. "Lord, I want to thank You that You are supplying all my needs. Thank You that You are Jehovah Jireh; the Lord my Provider." You may not feel well, but instead of complaining, say, "Lord, thank You that I'm getting healthier, stronger, better every day." Praise gets God's attention, not complaining.

April 16

God Knows Already

"Lord," Ananias answered, "I have heard many reports about this man and all the harm he has done to your holy people in Jerusalem."

ACTS 9:13

When Saul of Tarsus was blinded by the great light on the road to Damascus, God spoke to Ananias to go pray for him. But Ananias immediately reminded the Lord that he'd heard that Saul was very dangerous. Nevertheless, the Lord said, "Go."

If you're always telling God what you've heard, you're going to miss out on God's blessings. You'll get discouraged. Doubt will fill your mind. "God, the financial report says I'm never going to get ahead." Here's a key: Don't tell God what you've heard. God says you're the head and not the tail. Now don't tell Him all the reasons why you're not. Don't take your problems to God; take your praise to God. "Lord, thank You that I'm coming into my seventh year, a year of release, a year of abundance."

Announce It

The Spirit of the Sovereign LORD...
has anointed me to proclaim...
freedom for the captives and release
from darkness for the prisoners...

ISAIAH 61:1

Isaiah was saying in effect, "It may look permanent, but I'm announcing your freedom. I'm announcing you're coming out of debt...that sickness is not going to defeat you...new levels are in your future." Then he took it one step further. He said, "I'm declaring the Year of God's Favor." Notice this principle: He announced it, then he declared it.

What if we would do the same thing? "I'm announcing today we're coming out of debt, struggle, and not getting ahead. I'm declaring we're coming into increase, overflow, and abundance." Or how about this? "I'm announcing, 'We will not live negative, depressed, worried, anxious, or stressed out.' I'm declaring, 'We are happy, content, confident, secure, full of joy, and loving our lives.'" You have to announce it and declare it by faith.

Freedom

*It is for freedom that Christ
has set us free. Stand firm, then,
and do not let yourselves be
burdened again by a yoke of slavery.*

GALATIANS 5:1

Too often we're announcing and declaring the wrong things. "I don't think I can ever get these credit card payments down." That's announcing defeat and declaring mediocrity. You have to change what's coming out of your mouth. Start announcing freedom from anything that is holding you back. Freedom from loneliness...from depression...from addictions... from constantly struggling. It may not be true at the moment, but this is what faith is all about.

You may have struggled in an area for a long time, but let me declare this over you: "It is not permanent. I believe and declare God is releasing you into your seventh year. He is releasing you into opportunity, into favor; releasing you into healing, into breakthroughs. He is releasing you into the fullness of your destiny."

Created
in His Image

So God created mankind in his own image, in the image of God he created them; male and female he created them.

GENESIS 1:27

Archie Manning was a tremendous NFL quarterback, and two of his sons, Peyton and Eli, have also been great quarterbacks. How could that be? Out of the millions of young men who play football, how can these two brothers stand out? It's not a coincidence. They have their father's DNA.

When God created you in His image, He put a part of Himself in you. You could say that you have the DNA of Almighty God. You are destined to do great things, destined to leave your mark on this generation. Your Heavenly Father spoke worlds into existence. He flung stars into space. Now here's the key: He is not just the Creator of the universe. He is not just the all-powerful God. He is your Heavenly Father. You have His DNA. Imagine what you can do.

Created for Greatness

Now thanks be to God who always leads us in triumph in Christ, and through us diffuses the fragrance of His knowledge in every place.

2 CORINTHIANS 2:14 NKJV

Too many times we don't realize who we are. We focus on our weaknesses, what we don't have, the mistakes we've made, and the family we come from. We end up settling for mediocrity when we were created for greatness. If you're going to break out of average, you need to remind yourself, "I have the DNA of the Most High God. Greatness is in my genes. I come from a bloodline of champions."

When you realize who you are, you won't go around intimidated and insecure, thinking, *I'm lacking. I'm not that talented. I come from the wrong family.* No, you come from the right family. Your Father created it all. It changes your thinking from, *I'm unlucky. I never get any good breaks,* to *I have the favor of God. Blessings are chasing me down.*

One of a Kind

See what great love the Father has lavished on us,
that we should be called children of God!
And that is what we are!

1 JOHN 3:1

When you know who you are as a child of God, you'll start thinking like a winner, talking like a winner, and carrying yourself like you are a winner. You'll go from tossing in the towel and saying, "This obstacle is too big. I'll never overcome it," to declaring, "I can do all things through Christ. If God be for me, who dare be against me?" You'll go from looking at your test score and concluding, *I'm an average student. All I can make are Cs,* to *I'm an A student. I have the mind of Christ.* You'll go from looking in the mirror and mumbling, "I don't have a good personality. I'm not that attractive," to insisting, "I am fearfully and wonderfully made. I am one of a kind."

Who's Your Father?

*Therefore, if anyone is in Christ, the new creation
has come: The old has gone, the new is here!*

2 CORINTHIANS 5:17

I remember an advertisement for DNA
testing that asked the question, "Who's
the father?" They can take your DNA, and
out of the billions of people on earth, the
chances of your DNA matching someone
who's not your family are so small that it's
inconceivable.

In a similar way, when you gave your
life to Christ, the Scripture talks about how
you became a new creation. You were born
into a new family. You entered into a new
bloodline. Imagine that somehow they
could take a sample DNA from your Heavenly Father, then a sample DNA from you,
and run all the tests. The good news is that
it would come back a perfect match. Proven
beyond all doubt, you are God's child. You
have His DNA. You come from a royal
bloodline.

It's in Your DNA

*"Do not be afraid,
little flock, for your
Father has been pleased
to give you the kingdom."*

APRIL

23

LUKE 12:32

Given the fact that your spiritual DNA is a match to your Heavenly Father through the new creation, don't you dare go around thinking that you're average. *I could never accomplish my dreams. I'll never get out of debt.* Are you kidding? Do you know who your Father is? He created worlds. There's nothing too much for you. You can overcome that sickness. You can run that company. You can build and support that orphanage. You can take your family to a new level.

Quit believing the lies that say, "You've reached your limits. You've gone as far as you can go." Start talking to yourself as a winner. It's in your blood. You're expected to succeed. You're expected to get well. You're expected to live debt-free. Why? Because of who your Father is.

Like Your Father

Yet you, LORD, are our
Father. We are the clay,
you are the potter; we are
all the work of your hand.

ISAIAH 64:8

In one sense, it's no big deal that I am the pastor of Lakewood Church. My father was a minister for over fifty years. This is all I had seen growing up. It's in my genes. In the same way, it's no big deal for you to accomplish your dreams or to live healthy and whole. It's no big deal for you to lead the company in sales. Why? Like Father, like son. It's in your spiritual DNA.

You didn't come from ordinary stock. You came from the best of the best. It doesn't matter what we look like on the outside, what color we are, how tall or short, how attractive or unattractive, or how many weaknesses we have. What supersedes all of that is that on the inside you have the DNA of a champion.

A Champion

25 APRIL

To them God has chosen to make known among the Gentiles the glorious riches of this mystery, which is Christ in you, the hope of glory.

COLOSSIANS 1:27

Championship racehorses have been carefully studied and carefully bred for generations. Before breeding, the owners will go back decades and study the bloodline of a particular stallion. They'll research his father and grandfather and study how long their strides were, how tall their legs were, their takeoff speed, their endurance. With all this information, they'll choose what they believe to be the perfect match. They understand winners don't just randomly happen. It's in their DNA. That's what sets these horses apart. They have generation after generation of champions on the inside.

When the little colt is born with wobbly legs and doesn't look different than any other colt that is born, the owners are totally confident, knowing that on the inside of that little colt he has the DNA of a champion.

In Your Bloodline

*"LORD, the God of our ances-
tors, are you not the God who is
in heaven? You rule over all the
kingdoms of the nations."*

2 CHRONICLES 20:6

APRIL

26

If you look back and study your spiritual
bloodline, you'll see your Lord and Savior
defeated the enemy on the cross. There's
victory in your bloodline. You'll see your
ancestor Moses parted the Red Sea. There's
great faith in your bloodline. David, a shepherd boy, defeated a giant. There's favor in
your bloodline. Samson pushed down the
pillars of a huge building. There's supernat-
ural strength and power in your bloodline.
Nehemiah rebuilt the walls of Jerusalem
when all the odds were against him. There's
increase, promotion, and abundance in
your bloodline. A young lady named Esther
stepped up and saved her people from a certain death. There is courage in your bloodline.

Now don't go around thinking, *I could
never break this addiction.* You come from a
bloodline of champions.

Born to Overcome

...for everyone born of God overcomes the world.
This is the victory that has overcome
the world, even our faith.

1 JOHN 5:4

You were born to overcome and live in victory. It doesn't matter what your present circumstances look like. That addiction didn't come to stay. Freedom is in your spiritual DNA. That sickness is not permanent. Health and wholeness are in your DNA. That family problem, strife, division; it's not going to last forever. Restoration is in your DNA. Lack, struggle, and barely getting by are not your destiny. Abundance, increase, opportunity, and good breaks are in your DNA.

Now when thoughts tell you that it's never going to happen, just go back and check your spiritual birth certificate. Remind yourself of who you are. When the thought intrudes, *You'll never accomplish your dreams. You'll never get well,* just reply out loud, "No, thanks. I've already checked my birth certificate. My Father's name is God."

Heirs of God

Now if we are children, then we are heirs—
heirs of God and co-heirs with Christ...

ROMANS 8:17

You have the right spiritual DNA. When thoughts tell you otherwise, don't get discouraged. Just keep checking your spiritual birth certificate. Keep reminding yourself of who you are. Keep declaring this truth:

"I know who I am. My spiritual birth certificate verifies what is in my DNA. That's found in God's Word. Am I supposed to live average, lonely, struggling, and always getting the short end of the stick? No, it says in the Psalms, 'God's favor surrounds me like a shield.' It declares, 'No weapon formed against me will prosper.' It says, 'The number of my days He will fulfill.' It states, 'As for me and my house we will serve the Lord.' It says, 'I will lend and not borrow. Goodness and mercy are following us. Good breaks are chasing us down.'"

"Abba, Father"

Because you are his sons, God sent the Spirit of his Son into our hearts, the Spirit who calls out, "Abba, Father."

GALATIANS 4:6

When my nephew Jackson was a little boy, every night at bedtime, after his mother, Jennifer, prayed with him, she would go through a list of superheroes, telling Jackson who he was. That was her way of speaking faith into him, letting him know he was going to do great things. She would say, "Jackson, you are my Superman, my Buzz Lightyear, my Power Ranger," and on and on. Jackson would lie there, a big smile on his face, taking it all in. One night it got very late and she put him to bed in a hurry. A few minutes later she heard this little voice hollering out of his room, "Momma! Momma, you forgot to tell me who I am."

Let me remind you that you are a child of the Most High God.

Who You Really Are

The Spirit you received does not make you slaves...rather, the Spirit you received brought about your adoption to sonship. And by him we cry, "Abba, Father."

ROMANS 8:15

A lot of people have never been told who they are. They've had negative voices playing over and over. "You're not talented. You're not going to ever get married. You'll never get out of debt. You've come from the wrong family." As long as those voices are playing, it will keep you from your destiny.

Maybe nobody told you who you are. Let me help you out. Almighty God says: "You're a child of the Most High God. You are strong. You are talented. You are beautiful. You are wise. You are courageous. You have seeds of greatness. You can do all things through Christ. You didn't come from ordinary stock. You're a thoroughbred. You have winning in your DNA. You are destined to do great things."

The Right Family

"This dear woman, a daughter of Abraham, has been held in bondage by Satan for eighteen years. Isn't it right that she be released, even on the Sabbath?"

LUKE 13:16 NLT

In the Old Testament, people understood the power of the bloodline more than we do today. God started the first covenant with a man named Abraham. Back in those days, the right to God's blessings and favor was limited to his bloodline—the Jewish people. In today's scripture, Jesus saw a sick woman and said in effect, "She comes from the right family. She's a daughter of Abraham. She has a right to be well," then He made her whole.

On another occasion, a Gentile woman begged Jesus to heal her daughter. Jesus said in effect, "I can't do it. You come from the wrong family." It didn't seem fair, but that's how powerful the bloodline was. In this case, though, despite her Gentile bloodline, Jesus marveled at the woman's faith and healed the daughter.

A Child of Abraham

If you belong to Christ, then you are Abraham's seed, and heirs according to the promise.

GALATIANS 3:29

When Jesus died and rose again, He made a way for all people to come to Him, both Jews and Gentiles. Don't go through life believing the lies that you've come from the wrong family. "Your mother was depressed. You'll always be depressed." You have entered into a new bloodline. If God was standing before you today, He would say, "Isn't it right that you should be released from this limitation, seeing that you are a child of Abraham?"

Friend, you have a right to be blessed, to be free, to be healthy, to be happy, and to be whole. It's in your DNA. Your natural bloodline may have some negative things in it, but the spiritual bloodline will always overpower your natural bloodline. The spiritual is greater than the natural.

Mighty Hero

*The angel of the LORD appeared to him and said,
"Mighty hero, the LORD is with you!"*

JUDGES 6:12 NLT

The Midianites had overtaken the people
of Israel. When the Israelites' crops
came up, the Midianites would go in and
destroy the produce. They were a bigger
and stronger nation. It looked as though
they would eventually drive the Israelites
away. There was a man named Gideon who
was hiding in the fields, afraid of the Midianites. An angel appeared to him and said,
"Mighty hero, the Lord is with you."

I can imagine Gideon looked around
and thought, *Who's he talking about? I'm
not a mighty hero.* Gideon wasn't strong
and courageous. He was just the opposite;
afraid and intimidated, yet God called him
a mighty hero. Like Gideon, you may feel
weak, but God calls you strong. You may
feel intimidated; God calls you courageous.
You may feel inadequate; God calls you well
able.

See What God Sees

For by You I can run against a troop,
by my God I can leap over a wall.

PSALM 18:29 NKJV

As was true of Gideon, you may think you're average, but God calls you a mighty hero. When you get up in the morning and the negative thoughts come reminding you of what you're not, telling you of all your flaws and weaknesses, dare to look in the mirror and say, "Good morning, you mighty hero." Let these thoughts play all through the day. "I am strong. I am courageous. I am who God says I am. I can do what God says I can do." You have to remind yourself of who you truly are. You are a mighty hero.

God sees the mighty hero in you. God sees the DNA of a champion. Now do yourself a favor. Get in agreement with God. Start seeing yourself as that mighty hero.

Like Royalty

The LORD turned to him and said, "Go in the strength you have and save Israel out of Midian's hand. Am I not sending you?"

JUDGES 6:14

MAY
5

Gideon's response to the Lord's promise was, "How can I do that? I come from the poorest family. I am the least one in my father's house." What was the problem? Gideon didn't know who he was. God had just called him a mighty hero.

If you allow the wrong thoughts to play in your mind, you can have the talent, the opportunity, the strength, and the looks, but you'll make excuses and talk yourself out of it. I love the fact that God not only calls you a mighty hero but even the enemy sees you as a king's son, a king's daughter (see Jud. 8:18). He knows who you are. Now make sure you know who you are. Carry yourself like a king, like a queen, like a mighty hero. You come from the right family.

What You Can Become

*And they replied, "They were
like you, each one of them
resembled the son of a king."*

JUDGES 8:18 AMP

When God called Gideon a mighty hero, up to that point Gideon had not done anything significant. He had not parted a Red Sea or defeated a giant. I can understand God calling him a mighty hero if he had done something amazing. But it seemed that there was nothing special about him—just an ordinary, insignificant man. But God saw something in Gideon that other people did not see. God saw his potential. God saw what he could become.

Later, Gideon was interrogating his enemies and asked them, "What did the men look like whom you saw?" They said, "They looked like you, like a king's son." Here, Gideon had felt as though he was the least, inadequate, and not able to. But even his enemies said, "You look like a king's son."

Who Made You?

7
MAY

But Moses said to God, "Who am I that I should go to Pharaoh and bring the Israelites out of Egypt?"

EXODUS 3:11

When God told Moses to go tell Pharaoh to let the people go, the first thing Moses said was, "God, I'm ordinary. Pharaoh is the leader of a nation. He is not going to listen to me." Moses forgot who he was. He didn't see himself as a King's son but as inadequate. He focused on his weaknesses, his limitations. He started making excuses. He said, "God, I can't go talk to Pharaoh. I stutter."

God said, "Moses, who made your tongue? Who makes the deaf to hear? Who makes the blind to see?" God was saying, "Moses, I breathed my life into you. I put My DNA on the inside. Quit telling me what you're not. I say you're a King's son." That's what God is saying to each one of us today.

Created to Soar

...but those who hope in the LORD will renew their strength. They will soar on wings like eagles...

ISAIAH 40:31

MAY 8

I heard a story about an eagle that was raised with a brood of chickens and acted like a chicken. But one day he saw an eagle soaring overhead. All his circumstances said, "You're just a chicken," but something deep on the inside said, "This is not who I am. I may be in a chicken coop, but I was created to soar."

Flapping his wings as fast as he could, the eagle crashed into the side of the chicken coop. His chicken friends laughed and said, "See, you're a chicken." But he didn't let that failure or the ridicule talk him out of it. He kept trying, and one day he lifted up out of that chicken coop and began to soar. With every breath he declared, "This is who I really am. I knew I was an eagle!"

You're an Eagle

*And we all, who with unveiled faces contemplate
the Lord's glory, are being transformed into
his image with ever-increasing glory,
which comes from the Lord, who is the Spirit.*

2 CORINTHIANS 3:18

Perhaps, like the eagle in yesterday's reading, you've been in a chicken coop way too long. Perhaps chicken has become ingrained in your thinking. Let me tell you what you already know. You're not a chicken. You're an eagle. Don't let that limited environment rub off on you. Don't let how you were raised or what somebody said keep you from knowing who you really are.

Check your spiritual birth certificate. You'll find you've been made in the image of Almighty God. He has crowned you with favor. You have royal blood flowing through your veins. You were never created to be average or mediocre. You were created to soar. Abundance, opportunity, and good breaks are in your DNA. Now get rid of a chicken mentality and start having an eagle mentality.

May 10

Made for More

Do you see a man who excels in his work? He will stand before kings; he will not stand before unknown men.

PROVERBS 22:29 NKJV

I know a young lady who was raised in poverty, got pregnant at age sixteen, and dropped out of high school. She had had a big dream for her life, but it looked as though the cycle of lack and defeat would continue. She went on welfare and found a job at a school cafeteria, earning minimum wage. But something deep down inside of her said, "You were made for more. You're an eagle."

She went back to school and got her GED. Then she enrolled in college, working during the day and going to class at night. She graduated from college with honors and went on to get her master's degree. Today, she is the assistant principal at the same school where she once punched meal tickets. That's what happens when you know who you are.

Rise Above

"Stand firm, and you will win life."

LUKE 21:19

You may feel like the young lady in yesterday's reading. You may have been taught to live like a chicken, but you must do what she did. Draw a line in the sand and say, "I may be in a limited environment, but I am not settling here. I know who I am. I am an eagle. I am a child of the King. I am a mighty hero. I am a thoroughbred. I have winning in my DNA."

Get up every morning and read what God's Word says about you. Remind yourself of who you are in Jesus Christ. If you do this, I believe and declare, you're going to soar to new heights. You're going to rise above every obstacle. You're going to set new levels for your family and become everything God has created you to be.

You Are His Temple

Do you not know that your bodies are temples of the Holy Spirit, who is in you, whom you have received from God?

1 CORINTHIANS 6:19

Too many people go around feeling wrong on the inside. They don't really like who they are. They think, *If I was just a little taller, if I had a better personality, if my metabolism was a little faster...*

But when God created you, He went to great lengths to make you exactly as He wanted. You didn't accidentally get your personality. You didn't just happen to get your height, your looks, your skin color, or your gifts. God designed you on purpose to be the way you are. You have what you need to fulfill your destiny. If you needed to be different in any way, God would have made you that way. You have to be confident in who God made you to be.

A Masterpiece

For we are God's masterpiece.

EPHESIANS 2:10 NLT

To be a masterpiece means you are not ordinary. You didn't come off an assembly line. You weren't mass-produced. You are one of a kind. Nobody in this world has your fingerprints. There will never be another you. If you're going to reach your highest potential, you have to see yourself as unique, as an original, as God's very own masterpiece.

God's creation is filled with magnificent scenes and things that I think of as incredible—sunsets over the clear blue ocean, the Rocky Mountains, the vast solar system and Milky Way. But God says His most prized possession is us. What makes Him most proud is us. He is saying to you and me, "When I made you, I breathed My very life into you. I created you in My own image."

A Prized Possession

The LORD your God has chosen you out of all the peoples on the face of the earth to be his people, his treasured possession.

DEUTERONOMY 7:6

You are God's most prized possession. Don't go around feeling wrong about yourself. Quit wishing you were taller, or had a better personality, or looked like somebody else. You've been painted by the most incredible Painter there could ever be. When God created you, He stepped back and stamped His approval on you.

Somewhere on you, there's a tag that states, "Made by Almighty God." So put your shoulders back and hold your head high. You are extremely valuable. When those thoughts come telling you everything that you're not, remind yourself, "I have the fingerprints of God all over me—the way I look, the way I smile, my gifts, my personality. I know I am not average. I am a masterpiece." Those are the thoughts that should be playing in our mind all day long.

Wonderfully Made

I praise you because I am fearfully and wonderfully made; your works are wonderful, I know that full well.

PSALM 139:14

People may try to make you feel average. Your own thoughts may try to convince you that you are ordinary. Life will try to push you down and steal your sense of value. That's why all through the day you have to remind yourself of who your Painter is. When you dwell on the fact that Almighty God breathed His life into you and approved you, equipped you, and empowered you, then any thoughts of low self-esteem and inferiority don't have a chance.

All through the day, instead of putting ourselves down, we should go around thinking, *I am wonderfully made. I am talented. I am an original. I have everything that I need.* I dare you to get up each day and say, "Good morning, you wonderful thing! You are fearfully and wonderfully made."

Your Painter

He is the Rock, his works are perfect,
and all his ways are just.

DEUTERONOMY 32:4

Years ago I was in a home that had many paintings. Some of them looked as if they had been painted by a child—very abstract, paint thrown here and there. When they mentioned they had paid over a million dollars for just one of those paintings, I thought, *Wow! That is beautiful, isn't it?*

Come to find out, it was an original Picasso. It dawned on me that it's not so much what the painting looks like; it's who the painter is. The value comes from its creator. In the same way, our value doesn't come because of our looks or what we do. Our value comes from the fact that Almighty God is our Painter. So don't criticize what God has painted. Approve yourself. You have been fearfully and wonderfully made.

Agree with God

For you created my inmost being; you knit me together in my mother's womb.

PSALM 139:13

MAY
17

How many of us are bold enough to say as David did, "I am amazing. I am a masterpiece" (Ps. 139:14). Those thoughts never enter into most people's minds. They're too busy putting themselves down, focusing on their flaws, comparing themselves to others whom they think are better.

Your Painter, your Creator says, "You're amazing. You're wonderful. You're a masterpiece." Now it's up to you to get in agreement with God. The recording that should be playing in our mind all day long is, "I am valuable. I am a masterpiece. I am a child of the Most High God." Could it be this is what's holding you back? Your recording is negative. Don't be against yourself. Change your recording. Start seeing yourself as the masterpiece God created you to be.

The Apple of His Eye

Keep me as the apple of your eye; hide me in the shadow of your wings.

PSALM 17:8

I read a story about a man who died in extreme poverty. After the funeral, a painting in his rundown apartment was discovered to have been painted in the 1800s by a famous artist and ended up selling for over three million dollars. That man lived his whole life in poverty because he didn't realize what he had.

In the same way, every one of us has been painted by the most famous Artist there could ever be. But if you don't understand your value, just like this man, even though you have everything you need, even though you're full of potential, you'll never tap into it. That's why every morning you need to remind yourself, "I am not average. I am not ordinary. I have the fingerprints of God all over me. I am a masterpiece."

A Crown of Honor

"You have made them to be a kingdom and priests to serve our God, and they will reign on the earth."

REVELATION 5:10

19 MAY

The Scripture talks about how God has made us to be kings and priests unto Him. Men, you need to start seeing yourself as a king. Women, start seeing yourself as a queen. Start carrying yourself as royalty. Not in arrogance, thinking that you're better than others, but in humility be proud of who God made you to be. You are not better than anyone else, but you are not less than anyone else.

Understand, your Father created the whole universe. When He breathed His life into you and sent you to planet earth, you didn't come as ordinary. You didn't come as average. He put a crown of honor on your head. Now start thinking as royalty, talking as royalty, dressing as royalty, walking as royalty, and acting as royalty.

Strong and Confident

"This is my command—be strong and courageous! Do not be afraid or discouraged. For the LORD your God is with you wherever you go."

JOSHUA 1:9 NLT

I was in England a few years ago. They were having a ceremony to honor the queen. When the queen walked into the room, you could feel the strength, the confidence, and the dignity. She waved at everyone as though they were her best friends. What's interesting is there were all kinds of important people in that room from around the world. And I say this respectfully, but the queen was not the most beautiful, the wealthiest, fittest, or most educated person in the room either. But by the way the queen carried herself, you would have never known it.

Why? She knows who she is. She's the queen. She comes from a long line of royalty. It's been ingrained in her thinking, *I'm not average. I'm not ordinary. I am one of a kind.*

Approved by God

*But to do this, you will need the strong belt of
truth and the breastplate of God's approval.*

EPHESIANS 6:14 TLB

No doubt some mornings when the
queen of England wakes up, the same
thoughts come to her mind that come to all
of us. *You're not as beautiful as...as talented
as...as smart as... Be intimidated. You're inferior.* The queen lets that go in one ear and
out the other. She thinks, *It doesn't matter
how I compare to others. I'm the queen. I have
royalty in my blood...generations of influence,
honor, and prestige.*

But a lot of times we think, *I can't feel
good about myself. I have this addiction. I
struggle with a bad temper. I've made a lot of
mistakes in life.* Here's the key: Your value is
not based on your performance. You don't
have to do enough good and then maybe
God will approve you. God has already
approved you.

Reign with Him

...if we endure, we will also reign with him.

2 TIMOTHY 2:12

If you and I could ever start seeing ourselves as the kings and the queens whom God made us to be, we would never be intimidated again. You don't have to be the most talented, the most educated, or the most successful to feel good about yourself. When you understand that your Heavenly Father breathed His life into you, you realize that you also come from a long line of royalty.

Instead of being intimidated, you can do like the queen. Just be at ease, be kind, be confident, and be friendly, knowing that you are one of a kind. Ladies, you may not be the most beautiful person, but be confident you're the queen. Men, you may not be the most successful, but stand up tall. You're the king. You are crowned not by people but by Almighty God.

Be for Yourself

Jesus replied, "'You must love the LORD your God with all your heart, all your soul, and all your mind.' This is the first and greatest commandment. A second is equally important: 'Love your neighbor as yourself.'"

MATTHEW 22:37–39 NLT

Jesus said that if you don't love yourself in a healthy way, you will never be able to love others in the way that you should. This is why some people don't have good relationships. If you don't get along with yourself, you'll never get along with others. We all have weaknesses, shortcomings, things that we wish were different. But God never designed us to go through life being against ourselves.

The opinion you have of yourself is the most important opinion that you have. If you see yourself as less than, not talented, not valuable, you will become exactly that. If you feel unattractive on the inside, you will convey feelings of unattractiveness. That's going to push people away. The problem is on the inside. You carry yourself the way you see yourself.

Extraordinary

Your beauty...should be that of your inner self, the unfading beauty of a gentle and quiet spirit, which is of great worth in God's sight.

1 PETER 3:3–4

A few years ago I met a young lady who didn't have a lot of what today's culture defines as natural beauty, but on the inside she had it going on! She knew she was made in the image of Almighty God and was crowned with favor. She may have looked ordinary, but she thought extraordinary. She carried herself like a queen and walked like she was royalty. She smiled like she was Miss America and wore her dress as though it was brand new from Saks Fifth. All I could say was, "You go, girl!"

What makes her so special? On the inside she sees herself as beautiful, strong, talented, and valuable. What's on the inside will eventually show up on the outside. Because she sees herself as a masterpiece, she exudes strength, beauty, and confidence.

Love Yourself

*Love others as you
love yourself.*

GALATIANS 5:14 MSG

People see you the way you see yourself.
If you see yourself as strong, talented,
and valuable, that's the way other people
will see you. That's the messages you're
sending out. But if you see yourself as less
than, not talented, and not valuable, that's
the way others will see you.

Perhaps if you would change the opinion you have of yourself, if you would quit
focusing on your flaws and everything you
wish was different, if you would quit comparing yourself to somebody else whom you
think is better and start loving yourself in a
healthy way, being proud of who God made
you to be, then as you send out these different messages, it's going to bring new opportunities, new relationships, and new levels
of God's favor.

Not a Grasshopper

"There we saw the Nephilim (the sons of Anak are part of the Nephilim); and we were like grasshoppers in our own sight, and so we were in their sight."

NUMBERS 13:33 AMP

When ten of the spies came back from the Promised Land, they saw how huge their opponents were. Notice they didn't say, "Those people insulted us. They called us grasshoppers." They went in with a grasshopper mentality. They said, "We were in our own sights as grasshoppers." That's what they conveyed. Here's the principle at work: "And so we were in their sight." In other words, "They saw us the way we saw ourselves."

You may feel that you don't have the size, the talent, or the education. That's all right. All that matters is Almighty God breathed His life into you. He created you as a person of destiny. He put seeds of greatness on the inside. Now do your part. Start seeing yourself as the masterpiece God created you to be.

Well Pleasing

And a voice from heaven said, "This is my Son, whom I love; with him I am well pleased."

MATTHEW 3:17

When God said these words, Jesus hadn't started His ministry yet. He had never opened one blind eye, never raised the dead, never performed a single miracle. His Father was pleased with Him because of who He was and not because of anything He had or had not done.

We tell ourselves, "If I read my Bible more or could break this addiction, I'd feel good about myself." You have to learn to accept yourself while you're in the process of changing. We all have areas we need to improve, but if you go around feeling guilty and condemned, that will not motivate you to go forward. Do yourself a big favor and quit listening to the accusing voices. The enemy knows that if you don't like yourself, you will never become who God created you to be.

❊

Excellence

Then God looked over all that he had made,
and it was excellent in every way.

GENESIS 1:31 TLB

In Genesis 1, God had just created the heavens, the earth, the sea, the animals, and Adam and Eve, then He pronounced it "excellent in every way." When God looks at you, He says, "You are excellent in every way."

You may think, *Not me, I have these bad habits, these shortcomings.* Get out of that defeated mentality. You may not be perfect, but God is not basing your value on your performance. He's looking at your heart. Now quit being down on yourself. Quit living condemned and dare to believe you are excellent in every way. Our attitude should be, *Yes, I may make some mistakes. I have some flaws and weaknesses, but I know God has already approved me. I am excellent in every way. I am His masterpiece.*

Celebrate

Each one should test his own actions. Then he can take pride in himself, without comparing himself to somebody else, for each one should carry his own load.

GALATIANS 6:4–5

I know people who are good at celebrating others. They'll compliment their friends and brag on a cousin. And that's good. We should celebrate others, but make sure you also celebrate yourself. Be bold enough to celebrate who God made you to be. There is something special about you. Don't put others on a pedestal to the point where you think, *They are so great, and I am so less than.*

They may have more natural beauty or more talent in some area, but God didn't leave anybody out. You have something that they don't have. You're good at something that they're not good at. It's fine to celebrate them and say, "Look how great they are," as long as you follow it up by saying internally, "And you know what? I'm great, too."

Your Value

For the LORD takes delight in his people; he crowns the humble with victory.

PSALM 149:4

I heard about a mayor of a small town who was in a parade, riding in a float down Main Street with his wife next to him. When he spotted his wife's former boy-friend in the crowd, who ran the local gas station, he whispered to his wife, "Aren't you glad you didn't marry him? You'd be working at a gas station." She whispered back, "No. If I would've married him, he'd be the mayor."

You have to know who you are. God breathed His life into you. You have royalty in your blood. You are excellent in every way. You are not ordinary. You are a mas-terpiece. Get up every morning and remind yourself of who your Painter is. Your value doesn't come because of who you are. It comes because of whose you are.

In the Meantime

The LORD is my shepherd;
I have all that I need.

PSALM 23:1 NLT

31 MAY

It's good to have dreams and goals. We should be stretching our faith. But here's the key: While we're waiting for promises to come to pass, we shouldn't be discontent where we are. Maybe you're believing to have a baby, believing for a new house, or believing to get married. That's great, but don't go the next five years discontent if it hasn't come to pass. Learn to enjoy the season that you're in.

Being unhappy, frustrated, and wondering if something is ever going to change is not going to make it happen any sooner. When we're discontent, we're dishonoring God. We're so focused on what we want that we're taking for granted what we have. The right attitude is, *God, I'm believing for this, but in the meantime I'm happy with what I have.*

Learn Contentment

I have learned in whatever state I am, to be content: I know how to be abased, and I know how to abound.

PHILIPPIANS 4:11–12 NKJV

The apostle Paul said he had to *learn* to be content. It doesn't happen automatically. It's a choice we have to make. Being content doesn't mean that we don't want change, that we give up on our dreams, or that we settle where we are. It means we're not frustrated and fighting everything. We're trusting God's timing. We know He is working behind the scenes, and at the right time He will get us to where we're supposed to be.

Some situations will not change until we change, such as when we're frustrated, thinking, *Why is it taking so long? Why is my husband still aggravating me?* If God has us there, we must need it. He is going to use it to do a work in us. When we're content, we're growing, developing character, and being strengthened.

Choose to Be Happy

*...for it is God who works in you to will
and to act in order to fulfill his good purpose.*

PHILIPPIANS 2:13

There's something wrong if we're always discontented. "I don't like my job. I'm tired of this small apartment. These kids get on my nerves." That's going to keep you where you are. God's plan for our life is not to just make us comfortable but to grow us up, to mature us, so He can release more of His favor. You may not like where you are, but you wouldn't be there unless God had a purpose for it.

You don't grow as much when everything is going your way. You grow when there's pressure and you choose to be happy. You could easily complain, but you say, "Lord, thank You for another great day." All your dreams haven't come to pass, but you choose to enjoy the season that you're in. That's passing the test.

Always Give Thanks

...give thanks in all circumstances;
for this is God's will for you in Christ Jesus.

1 THESSALONIANS 5:18

David spent years in the lonely fields taking care of his father's sheep. What's interesting is that he had already been chosen and anointed to be the next king of Israel. David could have thought, *God, You promised me great things. What am I doing stuck out here with a bunch of sheep?*

But David knew that God was in control, so he just kept being his best, going to work with a good attitude, grateful for where he was. Because he was content in the shepherds' fields, he made it to the throne. But if you're not content in the season you're in, even if your dreams do come to pass, you're still not going to be satisfied. Here's the problem: Discontentment will follow you everywhere you go.

See the Good

Let your conduct be without covetousness; be content with such things as you have. For He Himself has said, "I will never leave you nor forsake you."

HEBREWS 13:5 NKJV

Discontentment is like a faint high-pitched sound coming from a cell phone—it follows us around. If God blesses us with a promotion, we're happy for a little while, but then the discontentment comes. We don't want to work so hard or we don't want the responsibility. But it's not our circumstances. It's the spirit of discontentment, complaining about what we don't like, never having enough.

That's why Paul said, "I've *learned* how to be content." You have to train your mind to see the good, to be grateful for what you have. Life will go so much better if you will be content in each season. Content when you have a lot, and content when you don't have a lot. Content whether you're in maintenance or management.

Grace for Each Season

*There is a time for everything,
and a season for every
activity under the heavens...*

ECCLESIASTES 3:1

You have the grace you need to enjoy each season of your life. If your dreams are not coming to pass, that's a test. Will you do as David did in the shepherds' fields and bloom where you're planted? Will you choose to enjoy that season and not just endure it, thinking, *God, when is this ever going to change? I've been praying for two years.* Maybe it's going to change when you change. You have to be satisfied with where God has you right now.

It doesn't mean you settle there and never expect anything better. It means you don't live frustrated, always wanting something more. "I need more money and a better job and a bigger house." "I need to lose twenty pounds." "I need my kids to make better grades. Then I'll enjoy life."

Find Satisfaction

*A person can do nothing
better than to eat and drink
and find satisfaction in their
own toil. This too, I see,
is from the hand of God...*

ECCLESIASTES 2:24

I know single people who are not going to
be content until they get married, and
I know married people who are unhappy
and wish they were married to somebody
else. Even if you accomplish your wish list,
something else will come up to make you
discontented. You have to put your foot
down and say, "That's it. Everything may
not be perfect in my life. All my dreams
may not have come to pass yet, but I'm not
living frustrated and stressed out. I'm going
to bloom right where I'm planted."

In other words, "I'm content whether
I'm driving a twenty-year-old Volkswagen
or a brand-new Mercedes-Benz." "I'm content whether I'm living in a small apartment or a beautiful dream house." "I'm
content whether my business is booming or
whether it's a little slow."

Freedom in Contentment

But godliness with contentment is great gain.

1 TIMOTHY 6:6

You cannot let your contentment in life be based on what you have or don't have, on who likes you or who doesn't like you. Learn to be content in every season. Life is very freeing when you can say, "I'm content with who God made me to be. I'm content with my personality, content with my looks, and content with my gifts. I'm content with where I am in life—my position, my career, my relationships, and my house."

While it's always good to be improving, you shouldn't always be wishing you were something different. It's a tragedy to go through life always dissatisfied, wishing you had more, wanting to look like somebody else, waiting to be happy. I'm asking you to be content right where you are with who God made you to be.

A Servant's Heart

"I am the Lord's servant," Mary answered.
"May your word to me be fulfilled."
Then the angel left her.

LUKE 1:38

Think about Mary, the mother of Christ. When she was nine months pregnant, she had to ride a donkey to Bethlehem. There was no hotel or hospital room awaiting her. It was swaddling clothes, or strips of cloth, rather than a new baby outfit. Mary didn't have designer jeans, a fancy purse, or a latte from Starbucks. But she never complained to Joseph.

And Mary didn't say, "God, if I'm going to have this baby for You, at least You could make it more comfortable on me." She was content in the season she was in, content when the angel said, "You've been highly favored," and content with a donkey and giving birth in a barn with a bunch of animals. It takes a mature person to be content on the mountaintop and content in the valley.

This Old House

*But if we have food and clothing,
we will be content with that.*

1 TIMOTHY 6:8

A couple of years after Victoria and I were married, we found a piece of property we really liked that had an old rundown house on it with major foundation problems. We decided to fix it up and live in it. The floors were so slanted that most of the interior doors would not close properly. That didn't bother us. We were happy.

My mother would come over to our house and say, "Joel, how do you live with these crooked floors?" But I've learned that God gives you the grace for each season. Today, we have a nice house with even floors. But I don't believe we would be where we are if we had not been content in that older house. It would have been easy to complain, but we made the decision to be content.

It's Your Life

As for me, I shall see Your face in righteousness; I will be [fully] satisfied when I awake [to find myself] seeing Your likeness.

JUNE
10

PSALM 17:15 AMP

A gentleman recently was telling me about everything wrong in his life and ended by saying, "Joel, I just don't like my life." Here's the problem: It's the only life you have. You may have a thousand reasons to live unhappy, but you have to make the choice that you're going to be content. If you're sour and complain, you'll get stuck. God does not promote discontentment. Focus on what's right in your life and what you do have.

Paul, who said, "I've *learned* how to be content," wrote much of the New Testament from a prison cell. When you've made up your mind to be content, prisons can't stop you, crooked floors can't stop you, donkeys can't stop you, lonely shepherds' fields can't stop you. God will get you to where you're supposed to be.

Getting You Prepared

*And let us not grow
weary while doing good,
for in due season we shall
reap if we do not lose heart.*

GALATIANS 6:9 NKJV

Every season is not springtime, with the beautiful blooming flowers, gorgeous sunshine, and cool weather. That's a great season, but there has to be planting seasons, watering seasons, and maintaining seasons, where you're pulling the weeds and tilling the soil. Those are important seasons. Without going through that process, you're not going to come into a new season of harvest.

Instead of being frustrated by difficulties, have a new perspective. That season is getting you prepared for promotion. It may look as though you're stuck, but God is at work, and at the right time the season will change. Winter always gives way to spring. It takes a mature person to be content not only in the harvest season but content in the planting season and in the "pulling the weeds" season.

Rejoice Today

This is the day the Lord has made. We will rejoice and be glad in it.

PSALM 118:24 NLT

12 JUNE

You may be in one of those difficult seasons right now, raising a small child, taking care of an elderly loved one, or perhaps dealing with an illness. It's easy to think, *As soon as I get through this tough time, I'll get my joy back.* No, this is the day the Lord has made. You have to choose to rejoice today.

God has given you not only the grace you need in order to endure this season—that doesn't take any faith—but to enjoy the season. When you're content, you see each day as a gift, appreciate the people in your life, and are grateful for what God has given you. That not only is developing your character, but you're passing the test. You will come out of winter, and you will come into your springtime.

Fully Satisfied

"I will fully satisfy the soul of the priests with abundance, and My people will be satisfied with My goodness," says the LORD.

JEREMIAH 31:14 AMP

JUNE 13

When I was growing up, there were five of us kids in the house. My parents didn't have a lot of money, but I always felt as though we were well off. We had fun. Life was good. We couldn't afford a family vacation every year, so every couple of months my father would take us kids out to the airport to ride the tram from Terminal A to Terminal B! We thought that was so great. Instead of complaining that he didn't have enough, my father learned to be content in each season.

When some of my childhood friends would tell me they were going to Disneyland, I thought that meant they were going to the airport to ride the trams. When I got old enough to realize what Disneyland really was, I needed counseling!

The Simple Things

...to put their hope in God, who richly provides us with everything for our enjoyment.

1 TIMOTHY 6:17

When our son, Jonathan, was about five and Alexandra was two, we planned a big vacation to Disneyland. It was a huge deal, and I was so excited for my children. But we weren't in the park fifteen minutes when Jonathan said, "Dad, I want to go back to the hotel and go swimming." I pled with him over and over, "We can go swimming anytime. We're at Disneyland!" But he refused to budge. I thought later, *I should have done what my dad did and taken them to the airport to ride the trams.*

You don't have to have a big vacation to have fun. Learn to enjoy the simple things in life—making memories with your family, playing hide-and-seek in the house, and watching the sunset with your spouse.

Now Is the Time

*...who satisfies your desires with good things
so that your youth is renewed like the eagle's.*

PSALM 103:5

A mistake we make too often is that we think that when we reach a certain goal—finish college, get the promotion, move into the new house, have a baby— then we'll be happy. The truth is that if you don't learn to be content where you are now, you won't be content when your dreams come to pass. Yes, you'll be happy when you accomplish your goals, but there are challenges that come along with it.

When God blesses you with a new house, it comes with a bigger yard to mow, more rooms to clean, more to maintain. The promotion means more responsibility. The beautiful baby means that three o'clock in the morning is feeding time. Don't pray for a bigger blessing if you're going to complain about a bigger burden.

This Moment

*"I came that they may have and
enjoy life, and have it in abundance
[to the full, till it overflows]."*

JOHN 10:10 AMP

Our church facility is a dream come true.
God did more than we could ask or
think. But with this amazing blessing came
an amazing utility bill. The first time I saw
it, I thought, *God, I sure liked our old facility*.
The good news is that God won't give us a
blessing if we don't have the grace to handle
the burden. Our part is to choose to be content.

You could be in one of the best seasons
of your life right now, but you're not enjoying it because you're focused on the burden,
on what you don't have, on how difficult
it is. Because you're waiting for things to
change, you're missing the beauty of this
moment, the joy of today. See the gift in
what you have right now. Don't miss it living discontent.

Embrace Today

There was no end to his toil,
yet his eyes were not content with
his wealth. "For whom am I toiling,"
he asked, "and why am I depriving
myself of enjoyment?"

ECCLESIASTES 4:8

I read a story about a man who lived his entire life feeling discontented, unfulfilled, and dreading to go to work each day, but who, when he arrived in Heaven, realized that actually he had been at the right place. Seeing his life from a new perspective, he realized he had made a difference.

Could it be that you're at the right place for the season that you're in, but you're not enjoying it? Maybe like him, if you would see it from a new perspective, you would realize that God is directing your steps. He knows where you are, what you like, and what you don't like. Instead of living discontented, embrace the place where you are. See the good. Be grateful for what you have. You have the grace to enjoy the blessing.

Stop Comparing

Always be joyful. Never stop praying. Be thankful in all circumstances, for this is God's will for you who belong to Christ Jesus.

1 THESSALONIANS 5:16–18 NLT

There is an underlying pressure in our society to be number one. If we're not the best, the leader, the fastest, the most talented, the most beautiful, or the most successful, we're taught to not feel good about ourselves. We have to work harder, run faster, and stay ahead. If a neighbor moves into a new house, instead of being inspired and happy for them, we think, *I have to keep up.* If a coworker gets a promotion, we feel we're falling behind.

If we're not careful, there will always be someone or something making us feel we're not up to par. We're not far enough along. As long as you compare your situation to others, you will never feel good about yourself, because there will always be somebody more talented, more beautiful, more successful.

Run Your Race

*Do you not know that in a race
all the runners run, but only
one gets the prize? Run in such
a way as to get the prize.*

1 CORINTHIANS 9:24

Don't make the mistake of trying to keep up with others, wondering, *Why can't I sing like that? Why can't I be the manager? When am I going to reach their level?* If you're not content with your gift, comfortable with who God made you to be, you'll go through life frustrated and envious, thinking, *I wish I had her looks. I wish I had his talent. I wish I owned their business.* No, if you had what they have, it wouldn't help you; it would hinder you. They have a different assignment.

You have to realize you're not running their race. You're running your race. You have a specific assignment. God has given you exactly what you need for the race that's been designed for you.

It's Not about Others

And let us run with perseverance the race
marked out for us, fixing our eyes on Jesus,
the pioneer and perfecter of faith.

HEBREWS 12:1–2

A friend, a coworker, or a relative may seem to have a more significant gift than yours. They can outrun you and outperform you. That's okay. You're not competing with them. You both have what you need for your assignments. Quit trying to outperform others, and then you'll start to feel good about yourself. Don't condition your contentment upon moving into a new neighborhood, having your business catch up to someone else's, or getting a promotion.

One of the best things I've ever learned is to be comfortable with who God made me to be. I don't have to outperform anyone to feel good about myself. I don't have to out build, outdrive, outrace, out minister, or outproduce anyone. It's not about anyone else. It's about becoming who God made me to be.

Different Gifts

We have different gifts, according
to the grace given to each of us.

ROMANS 12:6

I'm all for having goals, stretching, and believing big. That's important. But you have to accept the gift that God has given you. You shouldn't feel less than if someone seems to have a more significant gift. It takes a secure person to say, "I'm comfortable with who I am."

I hear ministers who have deep voices and are great orators, and I stand up in front of my congregation with my Texas twang. This is what I've been given. I can improve it. I can develop it. I can cultivate it, but my voice is never going to sound like James Earl Jones. There is always going to be somebody who can minister better, who is further along and more experienced. But that doesn't bother me. I know I have the gifts I need for my assignment.

Your Gift Is Significant

There are different kinds of gifts, but the same Spirit distributes them.

1 CORINTHIANS 12:4

JUNE
22

Quit discounting the gift that God has given you. It may seem insignificant, but you don't have to have a great gift for God to use it in a great way. Do you know what David's gift was that put him on the throne? It wasn't his leadership skills. It wasn't his dynamic personality. It wasn't his ability to write and play music.

It was his gift to sling a rock. He was a sharpshooter with a slingshot. He could have thought, *Oh, great. Big deal. I'm good with a slingshot. This is not going to get me anywhere. I'm out in the shepherds' fields, alone, no people. Just a bunch of sheep.* But it was his slingshot, that seemingly insignificant gift, that enabled him to defeat Goliath and eventually put David on the throne.

Use Your Gift

*Do not neglect your gift,
which was given you through
prophecy when the body of
elders laid their hands on you.*

1 TIMOTHY 4:14

You may not be as smart or as talented as someone else, but there's something God has given you that's unique, something that will propel you into your destiny, something that will cause you to leave your mark on this generation. Don't believe the lies that say, "There's nothing special about you. You don't have the right personality or the talent of your friend."

Similar to David, you have a slingshot, your gifting. It's not so much what you have. It's the anointing that God puts on it. That gift may seem ordinary, but when God breathes on it, you'll defeat a giant twice your size. You'll be promoted beyond your talent. You'll go places where you weren't qualified. You weren't next in line, but suddenly a door opened. Suddenly the dream comes to pass.

Titles Not Required

A man's gift makes room for him, and brings him before great men.

PROVERBS 18:16 NKJV

24 JUNE

Too often we pursue titles and positions, thinking we'll feel good about ourselves when we have them. "When I make it to sales manager, when I get on the varsity cheerleading squad, when I'm the head usher, the senior partner, the lead supervisor..." That's fine. But you don't need a title to do what God has called you to do. Don't wait for people to approve you, affirm you, or validate you. Use your gift, and the title will come.

If King David would have waited for a title, we wouldn't be talking about him today. When he went out to face Goliath, David wasn't a general, a corporal, or a sergeant. He wasn't even enlisted. He didn't have a title, a name badge, a uniform, or a single credential.

Just Do It

And Jesus grew in wisdom and stature, and in favor with God and man.

LUKE 2:52

Some people say, "As soon as they crown me King of the Office, I'll start being my best." It works the other way around. You have to show them what you have, then the approval, recognition, and reward will come.

When David saw Goliath, he could have said, "Nobody here recognizes my gifts, so I won't get involved." In fact, people were telling him he was not qualified. Neither bothered David. His attitude was, *I don't need a title or a position or their approval. God called me. He gave me this gift, which may seem insignificant. I'm not here to please them. I'm here to fulfill my destiny.* He went out and defeated Goliath. In a few years they gave him a title: King of Israel. Use your gifts, and the titles will come.

June 26

Use What You Have

So Samuel took the horn of oil and anointed him in the presence of his brothers, and from that day on the Spirit of the LORD came powerfully upon David.

1 SAMUEL 16:13

When my father was seventeen years old, he gave his life to Christ. He knew that he was called to preach, but his family was very poor, he couldn't afford to go to college, and he didn't have a position or title. His family told him, "John, you better stay here with us and pick cotton."

Daddy could have thought, *I feel this calling. I know I have something to offer if somebody was just behind me.* But he didn't wait for a title or for people to validate him. He started to minister in the seniors' homes, in the prisons, and on street corners. If you'll use what you have, as my father did and as David did, God will breathe on it. His anointing on that simple gift will cause you to step into the fullness of your destiny.

True Fulfillment

*"Here is a boy with five small barley loaves
and two small fish, but how far will they
go among so many?"*

JOHN 6:9

In the Scripture, there was a little boy who
had a sack lunch—five loaves of bread,
two fish. Nothing much. Yet, when thousands of people were hungry, Jesus took
his lunch, multiplied it, and fed the whole
crowd. We hear a lot about the little boy
being willing to give the lunch, but it all
started when his mother took time to make
the lunch. She used her gift that seemed
small to make a lunch, and we're still talking
about it today.

She was a homemaker raising a child
without a title or acclaim. But titles don't
bring fulfillment. Trying to impress all your
friends will make your life miserable, but
running your race, understanding your
assignment, and being comfortable with
who God made you to be is what brings true
fulfillment.

Your Gift Is Special

However, he has given each one of us a special gift through the generosity of Christ.

EPHESIANS 4:7 NLT

Don't discount the gift God has given you. It may seem small just making a lunch for your children, but you don't know how God is going to use the child for whom you're making the lunch. You may be raising a president, a world leader, a great scientist, an entrepreneur, a business leader, or a pastor. You may not touch the world directly, but your child may change the world. Your assignment may be to help your seed go further.

You may be gifted to play an instrument or sing. You may be gifted to teach children. Be secure enough to play the role that God has given you.

Understand Your Assignment

*There are different kinds of working,
but in all of them and in everyone it is
the same God at work.*

1 CORINTHIANS 12:6

Are you comfortable enough to not have to be number one, to be in the front, to have the title, the position, to keep up with others? We put so much emphasis on rising to the top, in being the leader. And yes, I believe in excelling and having big gifts and big dreams, but I also know that everyone can't be the leader. Everyone can't run the company. Everyone can't be on the platform. Somebody must open the doors. Somebody has to play the music. Somebody has to show people where to sit and where to park.

The beauty of our God is that He has given us all an assignment. Every one of us has a specific gift and purpose.

We're All Important

Each of you should use whatever gift you have received to serve others, as faithful stewards of God's grace in its various forms.

1 PETER 4:10

Who was more important in the miracle of the loaves and fishes? The little boy with the lunch or the mother who made the lunch? Without the mother, we wouldn't be talking about the miracle. Who is more important? As the senior pastor, am I more important than the ones who open the building? Without them, we couldn't get in. Or is it the ones who run the lights, the sound system, and the cameras? Or perhaps the ones who paid the bills during the week? Or maybe it's the ones who have supported the ministry down through the years?

Here's the point: We're all equally important. Without one, the whole thing wouldn't function properly. Be secure enough to play your role.

Be Who You Are

*There are different kinds of
service, but the same Lord.*

1 CORINTHIANS 12:5

It's easy to want what others have or to
do what they do, but if that's not where
we're called to be, if it's not where we're
gifted, we're going to be frustrated because
it's not happening. If we do get there, we'll
be frustrated trying to keep ourselves there,
because if you promote yourself and manipulate your way into a position, you will have
to constantly work to try to stay there. But
where God takes you, He will keep you.

When you're not competing, not comparing, not trying to be something that
you're not, life gets a lot freer. It takes all
the pressure off. And yes, I realize there
are some positions that carry more weight
and more importance, but in God's eyes the
usher is just as important as the pastor.

Fulfill Your Assignment

He who plants and he who waters are one [in importance and esteem, working toward the same purpose]; but each will receive his own reward...

1 CORINTHIANS 3:8 AMP

God is not going to judge you based on your neighbor's gift or your brother's gift or by how high you rose in the company. He is going to judge you based on the assignment that He has given you. Did you run your race? Not, did you outperform your neighbor, were you more successful than your cousin? You're not competing with them. They're running a different race.

Queen Esther was gifted to save her nation. The mother was gifted to make the sack lunch that was used to feed thousands. Two different assignments. Two different giftings. God is not going to say, "Esther, I'm prouder of you. You did so much more than the boy's mother who just made a little lunch." No, it's all going to be about whether or not we fulfilled our assignment.

——— ❋ ———

No Trading Places

Whatever you do [whatever your task may be],
work from the soul [that is, put in your
very best effort], as [something done]
for the Lord and not for men...

COLOSSIANS 3:23 AMP

A lot of times we think, *If I had their talent and if I could do what they're doing, I'd feel good about myself.* But the truth is that if you traded places, you wouldn't be happy. You wouldn't be fulfilled, because their gifts, their talents, their skills, and their personality have been uniquely designed for their assignment. You could try to do what they're doing, but the problem is the anointing on your life is for your gifts.

When you learn to accept your gifts, there is no competing, comparing, or wishing you looked different or had different talents. Just be the best that you can be with what you have and there will be a fulfillment, a satisfaction. God will open up doors. He will get you to where you're supposed to be.

Take the Pressure Off

I have fought the good fight,
I have finished the race,
I have kept the faith.

2 TIMOTHY 4:7

A few years ago I was out running. There was a man in front of me about a quarter of a mile, so I decided to try to catch him and started really pushing it. You would have thought I was in the final lap of the Olympic Games. I finally passed by him and felt so good that I beat him. Of course, he didn't know we were racing! And then I realized I had missed my turn and had to go back!

That's what happens when we're competing with other people, trying to outperform them and make sure we're more successful. We end up competing in a race that we were never supposed to be in. Take the pressure off. You're not really free until you know you're not competing with anyone else.

Join the Dance

As they danced, they sang: "Saul has slain his thousands, and David his tens of thousands."

1 SAMUEL 18:7

King Saul had been happy running his race until David started getting more praise than him. From that moment on, Saul never looked at David the same way and he ended up losing his throne over it. What was his problem? He couldn't handle somebody getting ahead of him. He was fine as long as he was number one, but he couldn't handle being number two. He got distracted and spent months and months trying to kill David, all because he wasn't comfortable with who he was.

Maybe like Saul you're at the one thousand level but you have a friend who's at the ten thousand level. The real test to see if God can promote you is, can you celebrate people who pass you by? Can you be happy for them and stay focused on your race?

Celebrate Yourself

*I press on toward the
goal to win the [heavenly]
prize of the upward call
of God in Christ Jesus.*

PHILIPPIANS 3:14 AMP

6 JULY

Friend, your race is run by one person—you. Don't get distracted with
competing against a neighbor, a friend, or
a coworker. Just run your race. Here's a
phrase I like: *Don't compare yourself.
Celebrate yourself.*

Celebrate what you've accomplished.
Very few people today can say, "I like
myself. I'm happy with my gifts. I am
satisfied with who God made me to be."
Remember, you don't have to have a great
gift for God to use it in a great way. It may
seem small, but when you use what you
have, God will breathe on it and do amazing
things. You will rise higher, your gifts and
talents will come out to the full, and you
will become everything that God has created you to be!

Under Your Feet

For he "has put everything under his feet."

1 CORINTHIANS 15:27

JULY 7

How we see our difficulties very often will determine whether or not we get out of them. When we face challenges and things come against us, it's easy to get overwhelmed and start thinking, *This is never going to work out. I'll just have to learn to live with it.* That kind of thinking not only pushes you down, but it stops God from working. It's going to attract fear, worry, and doubt. Many people settle for mediocrity.

You have to change your perspective. If you're going to live in victory, you have to see every sickness, every obstacle, and every temptation as being under your feet. It's no match for you. It's not going to keep you from your destiny. It's already defeated. It's just a matter of time before you walk it out.

Stepping-stones

*"You made them a little lower than the angels;
you crowned them with glory and honor
and put everything under their feet."*

HEBREWS 2:7–8

If you see your life challenges as being too big, that's going to cause you to feel weak, discouraged, and intimidated. You have to shake off the lies that are telling you, "It's too big. It's been this way too long. It's never going to change." All those challenges are under your feet. You're going to put a stop to it. It's just a matter of time before you break through to a new level.

This is a new day. God is saying, "Every enemy, every sickness, every obstacle; it's not going to defeat you. It's going to promote you." It was meant to be a stumbling block to keep you down. God is going to use it as a stepping-stone to take you higher. Keep the right perspective. It's under your feet.

Look Down in Triumph

In his unfailing love, my God will stand with me.
He will let me look down in triumph
on all my enemies.

PSALM 59:10 NLT

David faced all kinds of enemies and looked down on them in triumph. Notice that David did not say "*some* of my enemies." No, "*all* my enemies."

You may be facing a sickness or a financial difficulty that doesn't look or feel like it's under your feet. But we walk by faith and not by sight. In the natural, it may look huge, but when you talk to those obstacles by faith, as David did, you need to look down. When you talk to God, you should look up to ask for help. But when you talk to sickness or fear or depression, look down. It's under your feet. I've heard it said, "If you want to say something to the enemy, write it on the bottom of your shoe, because he is under your feet."

It's No Match for You

And God raised us up with Christ and seated us with him in the heavenly realms in Christ Jesus...

EPHESIANS 2:6

On the day before a big boxing match, the two fighters will come out at a press conference and stand toe to toe with their faces just inches apart. They'll look each other in the eye and just stand there and stare, trying to intimidate each other. They're saying, "I'm bigger, stronger, tougher, meaner. You're not going to defeat me!"

When you face a sickness, a bad habit, or an unfair situation, you don't stand toe to toe to look that enemy in the eye. That enemy is not at your level. It may seem so tough that you can't defeat it. But the truth is, it's no match for you. For you to look that enemy in the eye, look down under your feet. The enemy has limited power. God has all power.

Tread On

"Behold, I have given you authority to tread on serpents and scorpions, and over all the power of the enemy, and nothing shall hurt you."

LUKE 10:19 ESV

If God be for you, who dare be against you? Quit telling yourself, "I'll always struggle in this area. I'll never lose this weight. I'll never get out of debt." Change your perspective. You are not weak, defeated, or inferior. You are full of "can do" power. The same Spirit that raised Christ from the dead lives on the inside of you. Greater is He that's in you than he that comes against you. You are more than a conqueror.

Now start putting things under your feet. Think of that word *tread*. One translation says "to trample." If you will see these obstacles as being under your feet, as being already defeated, a new boldness will rise up. Your faith will activate God's power in a new way.

Fight the Good Fight

Fight the good fight of the faith. Take hold of the eternal life to which you were called...

1 TIMOTHY 6:12

I know a lady in her early thirties who was so shocked to be diagnosed with cancer that her personality changed. She became very depressed. All she thought about was how she might not make it. I told her, "You have to start looking down at that cancer. In the natural, it may be huge, but switch over to your eyes of faith. You and God are a majority. It was never meant to be a stumbling block. It was meant to be a stepping-stone."

She changed her perspective. She got her fire back, her passion back. She started fighting the good fight of faith. Today, she is four years cancer-free, married, and so happy. But had she not seen the obstacle as being under her feet, I don't believe it would have turned out that way.

Joy Is Your Strength

"Do not grieve, for the joy of the LORD is your strength."

NEHEMIAH 8:10

When David faced the giant Goliath, the first thing David said was, "I will defeat you and feed your head to the birds of the air." That's one of those enemies David looked down on as under his feet. By faith, he saw a giant as being smaller.

If we let life overwhelm us with worry and stress, that not only affects us mentally; it affects us physically. It weakens our immune system. The Scripture says joy is an emotion, and yet it creates strength. When you're in tough times, you have to shake off the worry, shake off the self-pity, shake off the disappointment. Get your joy back. That enemy, that sickness, that obstacle—it's under your feet. It's not going to defeat you. It's going to promote you.

Armed for Battle

*"You have armed me with strength for the battle;
you have subdued my enemies under my feet."*

2 SAMUEL 22:40 NLT

God knows every temptation and every obstacle you will ever face. He has not only put it under your feet, but He has armed you with strength for that battle. The greatest force in the universe is breathing in your direction. Tap into that power. Start declaring, "I am well able. I can do all things through Christ. I am strong in the Lord." When you do that, you're getting stronger and gaining energy.

We've all seen the sign in the post office of the "10 Most Wanted." Under their photos it says, "Armed and dangerous." If the enemy had a post office, your picture would be up there. The Most High God has infused "can do" power into you. You have to start seeing yourself as being armed and dangerous.

JULY 15

—❊—

Power Up

Put on the full armor of God, so that you can take your stand against the devil's schemes.

EPHESIANS 6:11

When we get out of bed in the morning, the first thing we should do is power up. Get our minds going in the right direction. Remind yourself: "I'm ready for this day. I am equipped. I am empowered. I have my armor on. I have my shoes of peace. I'm not going to get upset. I'm not going to let people steal my joy. I'm not going to fight battles that aren't between me and my destiny. I have my helmet of salvation. I know I am forgiven. I am redeemed. I am approved by Almighty God. I've been handpicked by the Creator of the universe. I have my shield of faith."

What are we doing? Powering up, getting prepared for a blessed, victorious, faith-filled day.

Every Thought Captive

We demolish arguments and every pretension that sets itself up against the knowledge of God, and we take captive every thought to make it obedient to Christ.

2 CORINTHIANS 10:5

JULY

16

You may be facing things that could easily steal your joy—a challenge in a relationship, a child not doing right, or an unfair situation at work. You could live stressed, uptight, and not sleep at night. Quit telling yourself, "This is too much. I can't handle it."

All through the day, especially when you're tempted to worry, you need to remind yourself: "This is under my feet. God is in control. It is not going to keep me from my destiny. I'm expecting great things. I'm expecting to have an amazing year. I have my sword of the Spirit; I'm speaking God's Word. I know every enemy is under my feet. I've been armed with strength for this battle." Come back to that place of peace.

Put Your Feet Up

JULY
17

*The LORD says to my lord:
"Sit at my right hand until
I make your enemies a
footstool for your feet."*

PSALM 110:1

hat do you do with a footstool? You put your feet up on it and rest. When we face difficulties, too often we take matters into our own hands. We get all worked up, thinking, *They did me wrong. I'm going to pay them back.* Or our medical report is not good. We can't sleep at night. We're so uptight.

But if you want God to make your enemy your footstool, you have to be still and know that He is God. When you're living upset and trying to force things to happen, God is going let you do it on your own. It takes faith to say, "God, I know You are fighting my battles. You promised it would work out for my good. So I'm going to keep my joy and stay in peace."

Stay in Peace

"You will not have to fight this battle. Take up your positions; stand firm and see the deliverance the LORD will give you, Judah and Jerusalem."

2 CHRONICLES 20:17

In yesterday's reading we noted that God will take those things that seem as though they're over you, and He will bring them under your feet as your footstool. When something is a footstool, you could say it serves you. It makes life easier. That's the way God is. When you stay in peace, God will take what's meant for harm and use it to your advantage.

Maybe at work somebody is not treating you right. They're playing politics, not giving you the credit you deserve. Don't get upset. Just keep being your best each day. Stay on that high road. Your job is not to straighten people out. Your job is to stay in peace. When you're in peace, God is fighting your battles. When you're at rest, God will make your enemies your footstool.

Your Vindicator

JULY 19

Then his brothers came and threw themselves down before Joseph. "Look, we are your slaves!" they said.

GENESIS 50:18 NLT

Joseph was sold into slavery by his brothers, then falsely accused by Potiphar's wife and sent to prison for something that he didn't do. Joseph did not try to pay people back or hold a grudge; he stayed in peace, and God turned it all around. The people who did Joseph wrong ended up working for him. His brothers came back and bowed low before him. Because he stayed in peace, God made his enemies his footstool.

God can vindicate you better than you can vindicate yourself. If you will let God do it His way, it will be bigger, sweeter, more rewarding, and more honoring. God can take the very people who are trying to push you down, the people who are trying to make you look bad, and He can use them to promote you.

Let God Do It

So Haman...robed Mordecai, and led him
on horseback through the city streets,
proclaiming before him, "This is what is done
for the man the king delights to honor!"

ESTHER 6:11

In the Scripture, Haman tried to push down Mordecai, who was Esther's cousin. He disrespected Mordecai and tried to make him look bad. But one day the king told Haman to get a royal robe, put it on Mordecai, and announce to everyone in the streets what a great man Mordecai was. The king specifically chose Haman to honor Mordecai, the very one who was trying to make him look bad.

That's what happens when you let God do it His way. That boss at the office who's not giving you credit; don't worry about it. You're not working unto people. You're working unto God. God is keeping all the records. Perhaps instead of you working for that boss, one day that boss may be working for you. Stay in peace. God can make your enemies your footstool.

God Doesn't Forget

*For the LORD will vindicate his people and
have compassion on his servants.*

PSALM 135:14

I have a friend who always gave his best effort at work, but for some reason the owner of the company didn't like him. Although he didn't get bitter or try to prove to everyone who he was, eventually his boss fired him. My friend then started his own real estate company and became extremely successful.

Several years later, his former boss was downsizing the company and wanted to move into a building owned by this young man. When he realized my friend was the owner and had to negotiate with him, he nearly passed out. Today that former boss is paying rent to the young man he once fired. That's God bringing justice. He doesn't forget what you are owed. He is going to make sure you get exactly what you deserve.

Dinner Will Be Served

*You prepare a table before me
in the presence of my enemies.*

PSALM 23:5

Stay in peace. God has your back. God will not only make your wrongs right, but God will bless you in front of your enemies. God could promote you anywhere, but He will give you honor, recognition, and favor in front of the people who tried to pull you down. One day they will see you receiving the credit that you deserve.

When that person who is lying about you tries to keep you from rising higher, imagine that God just turned the oven on. He is getting your dinner prepared. It's not going to be just you. Those people who tried to push you down, they're watching you get promoted. They said you don't have what it takes. They're watching you accomplish your dreams. Stay in peace. God has you covered!

A Position of Power

*The God of peace will soon crush
Satan under your feet. The grace
of our Lord Jesus be with you.*

ROMANS 16:20

All the things that come against us to try to get us upset—people talking, gossiping, spreading rumors, not giving you respect—are all distractions. That's the enemy trying to lure us off course, get us bent out of shape, and waste valuable time and energy on something that doesn't really matter. That's not a battle you're supposed to fight. Don't give that the time of day, and God will bring it under your feet.

When you're tempted to worry and get upset, just imagine yourself leaning back in a big comfortable chair, putting your feet up and resting them on top of that problem. You're saying, "God, it's under my feet. I know You are in control." When you're in peace, it's a position of power. When you're at rest, God is fighting your battles.

Unusual Favor

*He subdues peoples under us
and nations under our feet.*

PSALM 47:3

I know an American man who was trying to get his European wife a visa to
the United States. The man working at the
government office was very rude to him,
wouldn't give him any help, and said it
would take at least *five years* because they
were so backed up. This man was very frustrated, but he kept his cool and reminded
himself that by faith it was under his feet.

Several weeks later, he got a call from
the man. The visa was ready! He asked the
man, "I thought it would be five years?" The
man said, "It should have, but ever since
I met you, I can't get you off my mind—
morning, noon, and night. Take the visa and
go!" Friend, God knows how to make your
enemies your footstool.

It Shall Not Prosper

"...no weapon turned against you will succeed. You will silence every voice raised up to accuse you."

ISAIAH 54:17 NLT

Isaiah doesn't say that we won't have difficulties. That's not reality. It says, "Challenges will come. People may talk. You may get a negative medical report. A family member may get off course." God said, "The problem may form, but you can stay in peace, knowing that it's not going to prosper against you." Because you're His child, because you're in the secret place of the Most High, God has a hedge of protection, mercy, and favor around you that the enemy cannot cross. All the forces of darkness cannot keep you from your destiny.

When you face these challenges and you're tempted to worry, you need to tell yourself: "This problem may have formed, but I have a promise from Almighty God that it is not going to prosper."

The Final Say

*"Devise your strategy, but it will be thwarted;
propose your plan, but it will not stand,
for God is with us."*

ISAIAH 8:10

I read about researchers who were studying Alzheimer's disease. They studied the brains of older people who had died, both people who had and didn't have the disease. They found that many people who had lesions on their brains that technically qualified them as having Alzheimer's had never shown any signs of it when they were alive. Their reasoning was good. Their memory was sharp. Scientifically, they had Alzheimer's, but the symptoms never showed up. The common denominator is that they were positive. They were hopeful, and they stayed productive.

Just because the problem forms doesn't mean it has to prosper. We may have things come against us because of genetics, things that have been passed down. The good news is God has the final say. God can override it, so stay in faith.

A Future and Hope

For I know the thoughts that I think toward you,
says the LORD, thoughts of peace and not of evil,
to give you a future and a hope.

JEREMIAH 29:11 NKJV

When our friend Ramiro was born with no ears, the doctors told his parents, "He is never going to be able to hear or to speak." But Ramiro has parents who believe a weapon formed against us doesn't have to prosper. They prayed. They believed. They declared God's favor.

When Ramiro was just a few months old, the doctors discovered he had a very tiny start of an eardrum. These incredibly gifted doctors performed surgery, created new ears, and helped to correct the problem. Today, Ramiro can not only hear, not only speak, but he can sing. He helps to lead worship for our young adults. You may have heard him on *American Idol* singing "Amazing Grace" in front of millions of people. The problem may have formed, but it is not going to prosper.

Protected by Faith

But let us who live in the light be clearheaded, protected by the armor of faith and love, and wearing as our helmet the confidence of our salvation.

JULY
28

1 THESSALONIANS 5:8 NLT

Maybe you need to start putting things under your feet. You're letting that problem worry you and keep you up at night. God is saying, "I'll fight your battles, but you have to give them to Me." Come back to that place of peace. Don't let people or circumstances upset you. If somebody is not treating you right, God knows how to make your wrongs right.

Remember, when you talk to that sickness, that obstacle, or that depression, as an act of faith, do as David did and look down. If you will see these obstacles as being under your feet, God promises He will make your enemies your footstool. Instead of being a stumbling block, it will be a stepping-stone. You will defeat every enemy and become everything God has created you to be.

Overflow

You anoint my head with oil;
my cup overflows.

PSALM 23:5

God's dream for your life is that you would be blessed in such a way that you can be a blessing to others. David said that God is an overflow God. But here's the key: You can't go around thinking thoughts of lack, not enough, struggle, and expect to have abundance. If you've been under pressure for a long time and have difficulty making ends meet, it's easy to develop a limited mind-set. *I'll never have enough to send my kids to college.* That may be where you are now, but that's not where you have to stay.

God is called El Shaddai, the God of More Than Enough. Not the God of Barely Enough or the God of Just Help Me Make It Through. He's the God of Overflow. The God of Abundance.

God's Pleasure

Let them say continually,
"Let the LORD be magnified,
who has pleasure in the
prosperity of His servant."

PSALM 35:27 NKJV

God's people were supposed to go around constantly saying, "God takes pleasure in prospering me." It was to help them develop an abundant mentality. Your life is moving toward what you're constantly thinking about. If you're always thinking thoughts of lack, not enough, and struggle, you're moving toward the wrong things. All through the day, meditate on these thoughts: overflow, abundance, God takes pleasure in prospering me.

Don't you dare settle there with lack and not enough. That is where you are; it is not who you are. That is your location; it's not your identity. You are a child of the Most High God. No matter what it looks like, have this abundant mentality. Keep reminding yourself, "God takes pleasure in prospering me. I am the head and never the tail."

More Than Enough

"I will give it to you as an inheritance, a land flowing with milk and honey."

LEVITICUS 20:24

In the Scripture, the Israelites had been in slavery for many years. That was the land of Barely Enough. They were just enduring, surviving, barely making it through. One day God brought them out of slavery and took them into the desert. That was the land of Just Enough. Their needs were supplied, but nothing extra. But this was not God's idea of abundance.

God eventually took them into the Promised Land. That was the land of More Than Enough. The food and supplies were plenteous. The bundles of grapes were so large that two grown men had to carry them. It's called "the land flowing with milk and honey." *Flowing* means it didn't stop. It never ran out. It continued to have an abundance. That's where God is taking you.

August 1

A Place of Abundance

"Look at the birds of the air; they do not sow or reap or store away in barns, and yet your heavenly Father feeds them."

MATTHEW 6:26

You may be in the land of Barely Enough right now. You don't know how you're going to make it through next week. Don't worry. God hasn't forgotten about you. God clothes the lilies of the field. He feeds the birds of the air. He is going to take care of you.

You may be in the land of Just Enough. Your needs are supplied. You're grateful, but there's nothing extra. God is saying, "I didn't create you to live in the land of Barely Enough or Just Enough." Those are seasons. They are not permanent. Don't put your stakes down. You are passing through. God has a Promised Land for you. He has a place of abundance, of more than enough, where it's flowing with provision, not just one time, but you'll continue to have plenty.

August 2

Your Every Need

And my God will liberally supply (fill until full)
your every need according to His riches
in glory in Christ Jesus.

PHILIPPIANS 4:19 AMP

So often we look at our situations and think, *I'll never get ahead. Business is slow,* or *I'm in the projects. I'll never get out.* But it's not according to what you have; it's according to what God has. The good news is God owns it all. One touch of God's favor can blast you out of Barely Enough and put you into More Than Enough. God has ways to increase you beyond your normal income, beyond your salary, beyond what's predictable.

Quit telling yourself, "This is all I'll ever have. Granddaddy was broke. Momma and Daddy didn't have anything." Let go of all of that and have an abundant mentality. "This is not where I'm staying. I am blessed. I am prosperous. I am headed to overflow, to the land of More Than Enough."

Steps of Faith

You will eat the fruit of your labor;
blessings and prosperity will be yours.

PSALM 128:2

I received a letter from a young couple who grew up in low-income families that had accepted lack, struggle, can't get ahead, but not this couple. They had an abundant mentality and took a step of faith. On very average incomes, they decided to build their own house. They didn't take out a loan. Whenever they had extra funds, they would buy materials and hire contractors. A couple of years later, they moved into a beautiful house in a nice neighborhood, all debt-free. It was as though God had multiplied their funds. Not long ago they sold that house for twice what they had put into it.

The lady wrote, "My parents always told me that if I had beans and rice, that was good enough. But I always knew one day I would have steak."

Try It!

"I will open the windows of heaven for you. I will pour out a blessing so great you won't have enough room to take it in! Try it! Put me to the test!"

MALACHI 3:10 NLT

If you're going to become everything God has created you to be, you have to make up your mind that you are not going to just settle for beans and rice. You are not going to get stuck in the land of Barely Enough or the land of Just Enough, but you're going to keep praying, believing, expecting, hoping, dreaming, working, and being faithful until you make it all the way into the land of More Than Enough. Now there is nothing wrong with beans and rice. Nothing wrong with surviving. But God wants you to go further. God wants you to set a new standard for your family. He is an overflow God, a more than enough God.

God wants you to overflow with His goodness. He has ways to increase you that you've never dreamed.

The Fatted Calf

"And bring the fatted calf here and kill it, and let us eat and be merry..."

LUKE 15:23 NKJV

Jesus told a parable about a prodigal son who left home, blew all his money, and decided to return home. When his father saw him—the father represents God—he said to the staff, "Go kill the fatted calf. We're going to have a party." But the older brother got upset. He said, "Dad, you've never even given me a skinny goat."

Do you have a fatted calf mentality, or do you have a skinny goat mentality? You can survive in the land of Barely Enough. We can endure the land of Just Enough. "Just enough to make it through." But that is not God's best. Your Heavenly Father is saying, "I have a fatted calf for you. I have a place for you in the land of More Than Enough."

Special Delivery

*Now a wind went out from
the Lord and drove quail in
from the sea. It scattered
them up to two cubits deep
all around the camp...*

NUMBERS 11:31

When the Israelites were in the desert in the land of Just Enough, they got tired of eating the same thing every day. They said, "Moses, we want some meat to eat out here." They were complaining, but at least for a little while they had a fatted calf mentality.

Moses thought, *That's impossible. Meat out here in the desert? Steak for two million people?* There were no grocery stores, no warehouses to buy truckloads of meat. But God has ways to increase you that you've never thought of. God simply shifted the direction of the wind and caused a huge flock of quail to come into the camp. They didn't have to go after it. The food came to them. What am I saying? God knows how to get your provision to you.

Good-bye, Skinny Goat

They will not be disgraced in hard times;
even in famine they will have more than enough.

PSALM 37:19 NLT

One touch of God's favor can thrust you into more than enough. Don't talk yourself out of it. God has a fatted calf, a place of abundance for you. He is not limited by your circumstances, by how you were raised, or by what you don't have. He is limited by what you're believing. Maybe you've had that skinny goat with you for years and years. You've become best friends. You need to announce to him today, "I'm sorry, but our relationship is over. It's done. We're going to be parting ways."

He may cry and complain, "Baa-ah." He may ask, "Is there someone else?" Tell him, "Yes, I've found a fatted calf. No more thinking not enough, barely enough, just enough. From now on I'm thinking more than enough; an abundant mentality."

Generous Provisions

And God will generously provide all you need.
Then you will always have everything you need
and plenty left over to share with others.

2 CORINTHIANS 9:8 NLT

I talked to a lady who had been barely making it for years, but every Sunday she and her two sons were here at Lakewood. In spite of all the obstacles, she kept being faithful right where she was, honoring God, thanking Him that she was coming into overflow in her Promised Land.

This lady's son, from the time he was a little boy, always said that he was going to get a scholarship to go to college. He could have thought, *We're poor. I'm at a disadvantage.* But this mother taught her sons that God is a God of abundance. When he graduated from high school, he was awarded nine scholarships, totaling over 1.3 million dollars! His undergraduate, his master's, and his doctoral degrees are all paid for at Georgetown University.

Pressed Down

"Give, and it will be given to you. A good measure, pressed down, shaken together and running over, will be poured into your lap."

LUKE 6:38

What did Jesus mean by *pressed down*? It's like pressing down brown sugar in a measuring cup. When you do, you can put in about twice what it looked like initially. God is saying, "You're asking me for this, but I'm an overflow God. I'm about to press it down and show you My favor in a new way." After He presses it down, He is going to shake it together and not just fill it to the top. He is going to give you so much that you're running over.

That's the way our God is. Why don't you get in agreement and say, "God, I'm ready. I'm a giver. I have an abundant mentality. Lord, I want to thank You for good measure, pressed down, shaken together, and running over in my life."

Not Too Hard

*"Is anything too hard
for the LORD?"*

GENESIS 18:14

AUGUST

10

A friend of mine has a son who got his driver's license and really wanted a car. His father said to him, "Let's believe that God will give you a car." The son replied, "Dad, God is not going to give me a car. You can buy me a car." He said, "No, let's pray." They asked God to somehow make a way that he could have a car. A couple of months later, this man's employer called him in and said, "For the last two years, we've made a mistake on your paycheck. We've been underpaying you." They handed him a check for $500 more than the car they had been hoping to buy.

There is no telling what God will do if you'll make room for Him to show you His increase in a new way.

A Spacious Land

"So I have come down to...bring them up out of that land into a good and spacious land, a land flowing with milk and honey..."

EXODUS 3:8

Receive this into your spirit. God is bringing you into a spacious land. Not a small land. Not a little place. Tight. Crowded. Not enough room. No, it's a land of more than enough. A land of plenty of room. A land that's flowing with increase, flowing with good breaks, flowing with opportunity, where you not only have enough for yourself, but you're running over. Running over with space. Running over with supplies. Running over with opportunity. If you're not in a good and spacious place, my challenge is don't settle there. That is not your permanent address. It's only temporary. God is taking you to a good and a spacious land.

If you'll have this abundant mentality, I believe and declare you're coming into the land of More Than Enough.

Your Soul Prospers

Beloved, I pray that in every way you may succeed and prosper and be in good health [physically], just as [I know] your soul prospers [spiritually].

3 JOHN 2 AMP

AUGUST 12

Prosperity to me is so much more than having finances. It's having your health. It's having peace in your mind. It's being able to sleep at night. Having good relationships. There are many things that money cannot buy. But I also can't find a single verse in the Scripture that suggests we are supposed to drag around not having enough, not able to afford what we want, living off the leftovers, in the land of Not Enough.

We were created to be the head and not the tail. Jesus came that we might live an abundant life. We represent Almighty God here on this earth. We should be examples of His goodness—so blessed, so prosperous, so generous, so full of joy—that other people want what we have.

August 13

A Bountiful Harvest

*You crown the year with a bountiful harvest;
even the hard pathways overflow with abundance.*

PSALM 65:11 NLT

My father grew up extremely poor during the Great Depression and developed a poverty mind-set. On top of it, he was taught in seminary that you had to be poor to show God that you were holy. As a pastor, it took him years to being willing to receive God's financial blessings.

There is something on the inside of us that says we're supposed to be blessed. It's because we are children of the King. It was put there by our Creator. But here's the key: You have to give God permission to prosper you. You can't go around with a lack mentality, thinking, *God wouldn't want me to have too much. I'll just take the leftovers.* Get rid of that false sense of humility. That's going to keep you from an abundant life.

August 14

Lavished

*God will lavish you with good things....
God will throw open the doors of His sky
vaults and pour rain on your land...*

DEUTERONOMY 28:11–12 MSG

We think, *Is it wrong for me to want to live in a nice house or drive a nice car? Is it wrong to want funds to accomplish my dreams or wrong to want to leave an inheritance for my children?* God is saying, "It's not wrong. I take pleasure in prospering you." If it was wrong to have resources, abundance, and wealth, why would God have chosen to start the new covenant with Abraham. The Scripture also says, "Abraham was extremely rich in livestock and in silver and in gold." He was the Bill Gates of his day. God could have chosen anyone, but He chose Abraham—a man extremely blessed to be the father of our faith.

Give God permission to increase you. Give Him permission to lavish you with good things.

Produce Wealth

*But remember the LORD your God,
for it is he who gives you the
ability to produce wealth...*

DEUTERONOMY 8:18

David left billions of dollars for his son
to build the temple, and yet David is
called "a man after God's own heart." Get
rid of the thinking that, *God wouldn't want
me to have too much. That wouldn't be right.
That might not look good.* It's just the opposite. When you look good, it makes God
look good. When you're blessed, prosperous, and successful, it brings Him honor.

God wouldn't give you the "power to get
wealth" and then condemn you for doing
it. There is nothing wrong with you having
money. The key is to not let money have
you. Don't let it become the focus of your
life. Don't seek that provision. Seek the Provider. Money is simply a tool to accomplish
your destiny and to advance His Kingdom.

Be a Blessing

"May the LORD, the God of your
ancestors, increase you a thousand times
and bless you as he has promised!"

DEUTERONOMY 1:11

This is my prayer for you: A thousand times more favor. A thousand times more resources. A thousand times more income. Most of the time our thinking goes *TILT! TILT! TILT!* God is about to press some things down. He is about to make room for more of His increase. Now get up every morning and say, "Lord, I want to thank You that You are opening up Your sky vaults today, raining down favor, and lavishing me with good things. I am prosperous."

When you have this abundant mentality and a desire to advance the Kingdom, God will lavish you with good things. He will open up the doors of His sky vaults to where you not only accomplish your dreams, but you can help be a blessing to the world.

Redeem the Time

Walk in wisdom toward those who are outside, redeeming the time.

COLOSSIANS 4:5 NKJV

Time is one of the most valuable commodities we have. It's more valuable than money. You can make more money, but you can't make more time. To redeem the time means, don't waste it. Don't live this day unfocused, undisciplined, and unmotivated. We have a responsibility to use our time wisely. We're not always going to be here.

This day is a gift. Are you living it to the full? With purpose and passion? Pursuing your dreams? Or are you distracted? Indifferent? Just doing whatever comes along? Are you in a job you don't like? Hanging out with people who are pulling you down? That's not redeeming the time; that's wasting the time. Just like you spend money, you are spending your life. You're either investing it or you're wasting it.

A Gift Called "Today"

*But encourage one
another daily, as long as
it is called "Today," so that
none of you may be hardened
by sin's deceitfulness.*

HEBREWS 3:13

The first step in redeeming the time is to set short-term goals and long-term goals. What do you want to accomplish this week? What do you want to be five years from now? Do you have a plan? Are you taking steps to get there? Don't go another three years on a job you don't like, doing something that you're not passionate about. Life is flying by. This is your one shot. You don't get a do over. Once this day is over, you can never get it back.

God has given you a present. It's called "today." What are you going to do with it? This is a call to action. Get focused. Get organized. Set your goals. Make your plans. God could have chosen anyone to be here, but He chose you.

——— ❧ ———

Be "On Purpose"

Therefore see that you walk carefully
[living life with honor, purpose, and courage...],
not as the unwise, but as wise...,
making the very most of your time...

EPHESIANS 5:15–16 AMP

Paul said in effect that if you're going to reach your highest potential, you have to be an "on purpose" person. You know where you're going. You're not vague, distracted, waiting to see what happens. You're focused. You're making the most of each opportunity. Let me put it in more practical terms: Staying on social media for hours a day and catching up on the latest gossip is not redeeming the time. Playing video games for hours a day when you could be studying is not redeeming the time. Talking on the phone for hours a day to a friend who has no dreams is not redeeming the time.

There are a thousand things you can give your time to each day. You have to be disciplined to stay focused on what's best for you.

Get Organized

For God is not a God of disorder but of peace...

1 CORINTHIANS 14:33

The Scripture talks about living well spent lives. When we go to bed at night, we should ask ourselves, "Did I live a well spent day? Did I take steps toward my goals? Did I invest or waste my time?" I read that the average person spends over eighty hours a year looking for things they misplaced—car keys, cell phones, glasses, receipts, and children! Do yourself a favor—get organized and redeem that time.

I know too many people who are incredibly talented and have great potential, but they're not disciplined with their time. They have good intentions, but they're easily distracted and end up off course. They end up chasing the latest trend, trying to keep up with friends, distracted, entangled in things that are not a part of their destiny.

Entrusted with His Life

"My dear Martha, you are worried and upset over all these details! There is only one thing worth being concerned about."

LUKE 10:41–42 NLT

It's easy to get sidetracked by things that pull you off course, and when you finally look up, the day is gone, or the year is gone, or twenty years have gone. Nothing will be sadder than to come to the end of life and think, *Why did I waste so many days? Why didn't I live focused?*

Make this decision with me that you're going to redeem the time. We have a responsibility. God has entrusted you with His life. He breathed His breath into you. He's put gifts and talents on the inside. You're not just on planet earth taking up space. You're a person of destiny. With that gift of life comes a responsibility to develop your talents, to pursue your dreams, and to become who God's created you to be.

Run with Purpose

*I run with purpose
in every step.*

1 CORINTHIANS 9:26 NLT

On a regular basis, you need to reevaluate what you're doing. Refocus your life. Get rid of any distractions. Paul said every step he took was purposeful. When we understand the value of time and see each day as the gift that it is, it helps us to keep the right perspective. You realize every battle is not worth fighting. You don't have time to get engaged in conflicts that are not between you and your God-given destiny.

If somebody has a problem with you, as long as you're doing what God's put in your heart, with all due respect, that's their problem and not yours. You don't have to resolve conflicts with every person. Some people don't want to be at peace with you. Don't waste your valuable time fighting battles that don't matter.

Number Your Days

*Teach us to number our days,
that we may gain a heart
of wisdom.*

PSALM 90:12

When you realize your days are numbered, you don't respond to every critic. You don't try to convince people to like you who are never going to like you. You accept the fact that some people are never going to give you their approval or to be happy about you. But that's okay, because their happiness is not your responsibility. You know you have Almighty God's approval.

Always be kind and respectful, but your attitude should be, *If you don't want to be happy, that's fine, but you're not going to keep me from being happy. I know this day is a gift, and I'm not going to live it trying to change things that I cannot change or trying to fix people who don't want to be fixed.* That's redeeming the time.

What Is Your Life?

*What is your life? You are a
mist that appears for a little
while and then vanishes.*

JAMES 4:14

A lady was telling me about a family
member who had done her wrong. She
was very negative and starting to get bitter. I told her that life is too short to live
that way. Let it go, and God will be your
vindicator. She didn't want to hear it. She
said, "No, I'm not going to be happy until
he apologizes." I wonder how many days
that we've wasted doing similar things. We
can't say that we redeemed the time when
we just drag through our days being upset,
offended, and discouraged.

When you realize your time is limited,
you don't get offended. You don't get upset
because somebody's playing politics; you
don't get stressed out because somebody's
trying to make you look bad. You let it go
and trust God to make your wrongs right.

August 25

Blessed Sleep

"In your anger do not sin":
Do not let the sun go down while you are
still angry, and do not give the devil a foothold.

EPHESIANS 4:26–27

The reason many people have no joy or enthusiasm is because they go to bed each night with unforgiveness in their heart. They're reliving their hurts, thinking about their disappointments. Here's the problem: If the sun goes down with bitterness, it will come back up with bitterness. If it goes down with resentment, it comes back up with resentment. That's blocking God's blessings.

Before you go to bed each night, you need to say, "God, I'm releasing every negative thing that's happened to me today—every hurt, every worry, and every disappointment. I'm forgiving the people who did me wrong. God, I'm going to bed in peace." When you do that, the sun will go down with nothing blocking God's blessings. Don't go to bed at night with any kind of defeat still in your mind.

For Our Good

*And we know that in all things God
works for the good of those who love him,
who have been called according to his purpose.*

ROMANS 8:28

A local television reporter in Houston
got an assignment during Hurricane
Ike to find people who were down and out
and sad, but she only found people who
were grateful that they were alive and talking positively about how they were going to
make it. She thought her supervisor would
be excited that she got Victoria and me to
do an interview, but the station only wanted
sad stories. She ended up getting terminated
over that incident!

She could have been discouraged,
depressed, and bitter, but she understands
this principle that every day is a gift from
God. She started thanking God that new
doors were going to open and thanking Him
that favor was coming her way. Not long
after that, she was offered a dream job from
a prestigious broadcasting company.

Invest Your Time

Those who sow with tears
will reap with songs of joy.

PSALM 126:5

I've heard it said, "Disappointments are inevitable, but misery is optional." No matter what kind of setbacks you face, no matter who does you wrong, you don't have to drag through life defeated, depressed, and bitter. Start redeeming the time. Start thanking God that He's in control, that new doors are opening, and that favor is coming your way.

We all go through the valleys, but the valleys lead us to higher mountains. When you're in the valley, instead of sitting around thinking about your problems, go out and do something good for somebody else. When you invest your time the right way in helping others, those seeds that you sow will create the harvest you need, not to just get out of the valley, but to come up to a new level of your destiny.

Walk with the Wise

Walk with the wise and become wise,
for a companion of fools suffers harm.

PROVERBS 13:20

It's not only important how we spend our time, but with whom we spend it. To redeem the time may mean you have to prune off some relationships that are not adding value to your life. Don't hang around people who are not going anywhere, who have no goals or dreams, who compromise and take the easy way out. If you tolerate mediocrity, it will rub off on you. If you hang out with jealous, critical, unhappy people, you will end up jealous, critical, and unhappy.

Take a look at your friends. If your friends are winners, leaders, givers, and successful, if they have integrity and a spirit of excellence and are positive and motivated, those good qualities are going to rub off on you. Invest your time with them. They're making you better.

The Right Friendships

Do not be misled: "Bad company corrupts good character."

1 CORINTHIANS 15:33

The only thing that's keeping some people from a new level of their destiny is wrong friendships. You cannot hang out with chickens and expect to soar like an eagle. You don't have to go tell them, "Hey, I'm cutting you off." But you can just gradually spend less and less time with them. "Well, what if I hurt their feelings?" Well, what if they keep you from your destiny?

If you hang out with people who are sloppy, undisciplined, not motivated, and not going anywhere, find some new friends. You cannot become who God created you to be hanging out with them. They may be good people, and they may have good hearts, but your destiny is too great, your assignment is too important, and your time is too valuable to let them drag you down.

An Outgrown Friendship

Can two people walk together without agreeing on the direction?

AMOS 3:3 NLT

Here's a key as to why you need to reevaluate your friendships: If you don't let go of the wrong people, you'll never meet the right people. Sometimes we can outgrow a friendship. It was good at one time. For a few years, you were fulfilled. But now you've grown more than they have. You're running at a different pace. Your gifts are coming out in a greater way. That doesn't make them a bad person. It's just a new season.

Human nature likes to hold on to the old. We like to keep everything the same. But the truth is that it's healthy for seasons to change. It doesn't mean you can't still be their friend; you just know you cannot become all you were created to be unless you spend less time with them.

A New Season

As iron sharpens iron,
so a friend sharpens a friend.

PROVERBS 27:17 NLT

There are people who come into our lives who are like scaffolding. They're designed to be there for a period of time in our lives. (I'm not talking about a marriage situation; I'm talking about friendships.) They help us grow, inspire us, and motivate us. But at some point scaffolding must come off or else the building will never be what it was meant to be, and so must some people.

Appreciate the people who have helped you. Always honor them, but be big enough to recognize when their part in your story is over. On a regular basis, you need to reevaluate your friendships and the people with whom you choose to spend time. Are they in the right position? Has the position changed? Could it be that it's a new season?

Your Inner Circle

One of them, the disciple whom Jesus loved, was reclining next to him.

JOHN 13:23

When Jesus was on the earth, He was very selective with His friendships. Everyone wanted to be close to Him. But He chose only twelve disciples with whom to spend most of His time. Out of those twelve, three were his close friends: Peter, James, and John. One could be considered his best friend, John, the disciple "whom Jesus loved."

Be careful who you allow in your inner circle. You may have twenty people you call friends, but make sure the two or three you choose to be close to you are 100 percent for you. Make sure they believe in you and are with you through thick or thin. You may not be seeing God's best because you're investing valuable time in people who were never supposed to be a part of your inner circle.

Joined in Spirit

He did not let anyone follow him except Peter, James and John the brother of James.

MARK 5:37

In Mark 5, Jesus went to pray for a little girl who had died. When He arrived at the home, He didn't allow anyone to go in with him except for His inner circle. Why? Jesus knew when He got in that room where the little girl was dead, He needed people who wouldn't question who He was. He needed people who believed.

When you're in the heat of the battle, when you need a breakthrough, you need people who are joined in spirit with you. You need people who will say, "If you're bold enough to believe it, count on me. I'm bold enough to agree with you." "If you believe you can get your degree, or you can see your marriage restored, then count on me. I'm on board. I'm all for you."

Love from a Distance

*But they laughed at him.
After he put them all out, he
took the child's father and
mother and the disciples who
were with him, and went in
where the child was.*

MARK 5:40

In Mark 5, when the mourners of the little dead girl mocked Jesus, what He did next is a key to living in victory. It says, "He put them all out." Notice that the Son of God asked them to leave. He showed them the door. His attitude was, *I don't need your doubt. I'm going to surround Myself with people of faith who understand My assignment.*

If you have people close to you who are constantly pulling you down, telling you how you'll never accomplish your dreams, understand that it is scriptural to show them the door. It may be difficult, but you have to have the attitude, *I cannot fulfill my destiny with your critical spirit in my life. I love you, but I'm going to love you from a distance.*

4

Who's on Your Team

A friend is always loyal, and a brother is born to help in time of need.

PROVERBS 17:17 NLT

In Mark 5, Jesus demonstrated that who you have in your inner circle is extremely important. If Jesus went to the trouble to ask the wrong people to leave, if He was that concerned about His inner circle, how much more concerned should we be with who's in our inner circle?

Pay attention to who's on your team. Who's speaking into your life? To whom are you giving your time and attention? In practical terms, who are you eating lunch with every day at the office? Who are you talking to on the phone so much? Are they building you up or tearing you down? Are they pushing you toward your destiny, or are they telling you what you can't do? Are they modeling excellence, integrity, character, and godliness? You have a responsibility to redeem your time.

Better Friends

*As for my companion,
he betrayed his friends;
he broke his promises.*

PSALM 55:20 NLT

Sometimes we know a person's not good for us, we know they're dragging us down, but we think if we let them go, we're going to be lonely. Yes, you may be lonely for a season, but you'll never give up something for God without Him giving you something better back in return. God will not only give you new friends, He'll give you better friends. People who inspire you, celebrate you, and push you forward.

This may mean that you have to stay away from the person who's always bad-mouthing the boss; you don't need that poison in your life. You may have to stop hanging out with that neighbor who always has a sad song. It's better to make the change and be lonely for a season than to be poisoned for a lifetime.

A Well Spent Life

*Seventy years are given to us!
Some even live to eighty. But even the best
years are filled with pain and trouble;
soon they disappear, and we fly away.*

PSALM 90:10 NLT

When we come to the end of our days, God is going to ask us, "What did you do with the time I entrusted to you? Did you develop your gifts and talents? Did you accomplish your assignment? How did you spend your life?" It's not going to work to make excuses for why we did not redeem the time.

Make this decision that you're going to be an on-purpose person. Set your goals and be disciplined to stick with it. Prune off those relationships that are not adding to your life. And don't go to bed with any kind of defeat, bitterness, or negativity still in your mind. This day is a gift. Make sure you're investing your time and not wasting it. If you do this, you're going to see God's favor in new ways.

Created to Finish

*...looking unto Jesus, the author
and finisher of our faith.*

HEBREWS 12:2 NKJV

Starting is easy—a diet, school, a family. Finishing is what can be difficult. Any two people can get married, but it takes commitment to stick with it. Anyone can have a dream, but it takes determination, perseverance, and a made-up mind to see it come to pass. Too many people start off well. They have big dreams. But along the way they have some setbacks, get discouraged, and think, *What's the use?*

God has not only given you the grace to start; He has given you the grace to finish. When you are tempted to get discouraged, give up on a dream, give up on a relationship, or give up on a project, you have to remind yourself, *I was not created to give up. I was not created to quit. I was created to finish.*

Finishing Grace

Blessed is the one who perseveres under trial because, having stood the test, that person will receive the crown of life that the Lord has promised to those who love him.

JAMES 1:12

Maybe you're tempted to give up on a dream. Things haven't turned out the way you planned. It was going fine at first, but then you had some obstacles and you think, *It just wasn't meant to be.* Here's what I've learned. The enemy doesn't try to stop you from starting. But when you have a made-up mind and keep pushing forward, doing the right thing, taking new ground, he will work overtime to try to keep you from finishing.

Friend, you have the grace to finish. Quit talking defeat and start talking victory. "I can do all things through Christ. I am full of wisdom, talent, and creativity. I will pass this course." When you do that, finishing grace will help you do what you could not do on your own.

He Makes a Way

...walk in a manner worthy of the Lord,
fully pleasing to him, bearing fruit
in every good work and increasing
in the knowledge of God.

COLOSSIANS 1:10 ESV

What does it mean to tap into God's finishing grace? It means that when your friend turns on you, when you lose that client, when your child gets in trouble, you keep moving forward, thanking God that He is in control, thanking Him that He is fighting your battles. When you should get weaker, you get stronger. When you should be complaining, you have a song of praise. Instead of talking about how big the problem is, you're talking about how big your God is. When you should go under, God causes you to go over. When you don't see a way, He makes a way.

If you will keep moving forward in faith, honoring God, you will come into a strength that you didn't have before. That's finishing grace.

A Flourishing Finish

...being confident of this, that he who began a good work in you will carry it on to completion until the day of Christ Jesus.

PHILIPPIANS 1:6

Y ou may be up against challenges right now. Perhaps you're facing discouragement, having to shake off self-pity and what somebody said. It's because you are moving forward. You're making progress. Keep reminding yourself that God is the author and the finisher of your faith. He helped you to get started. That's great, but there's something more important: He is going to help you to finish. He didn't bring you this far to leave you.

One translation says, "He will bring you to a flourishing finish"—not a defeated finish, where you barely make it and are beat up and broke. You are coming to a flourishing finish, a finish more rewarding than you ever imagined. God is breathing in your direction, helping you to become who He created you to be.

The Finishing Line

God is faithful; he will not let you be tempted beyond what you can bear. But when you are tempted, he will also provide a way out so that you can endure it.

1 CORINTHIANS 10:13

SEPTEMBER

14

hen you're tempted to get discouraged and settle, it's because you're
your breakthrough. You're close to
he problem turn around. The good
on the way. The healing is on the
e contract is on the way. Now you
ap into this finishing grace. You've
far to stop now. You've believed
You've worked too hard. You've
too much.

eed to say, "God began a good
e, and He is going to complete
oing to keep honoring God. I'm
ep being good to people. I'm
ep on being my best." Every day
, you are passing the test. You
closer to coming into your fin-

Stay in Faith

Potiphar noticed this and realized that the LORD was with Joseph, giving him success in everything he did.

GENESIS 39:3 NLT

SEPTEMBER

11

As a teenager, God gave Joseph a dream that one day he would rule a nation. He had a big dream and life was good. But when Joseph was seventeen, his brothers sold him into slavery, and he was put in prison for years for something he didn't do. His whole world was turned upside down. He must have been angry and upset. But Joseph knew he had the grace to finish what God put in his heart. So he stayed in faith. He kept doing the right thing when the wrong thing was happening.

One day the Pharaoh had a dream that he didn't understand, which Joseph was able to interpret. Pharaoh was so impressed with Joseph that he put him in charge of the whole nation. Joseph's dream came to pass.

God Will Override

But the LORD was with Joseph
and extended lovingkindness to him,
and gave him favor in the sight of the warden.

GENESIS 39:21 AMP

God has put something on you that will override people being against you. It will override bad breaks and injustice. You have the grace not to just start. You have something even more powerful—the grace to finish. When you have an attitude like Joseph had, you cannot stay defeated. Life may push you down, but God will push you back up. People may do you wrong, but God will be your vindicator. Situations may look impossible, but God can do the impossible.

When you have finishing grace, all the forces of darkness cannot stop you. You may have some setbacks, bad breaks, and injustice. But don't worry. It's only temporary. It's just a detour on the way to your destiny. That's a sign that you are moving toward your finish line.

In It to Win

Keep your eyes open, h⸤
your convictions, give it ⸤
be resolute, and love wit⸤

1 CORINTHIANS ⸤

The enemy fights aga⸤ headed toward the ⸤ tinies, people who are ⸤ people like you who ar⸤ ishing finish. When th⸤ you have to dig your ⸤ in it to win it. I am n⸤ sition."

Our attitude sh⸤ up mind. *I am deter⸤ moving forward in ⸤ spite of the loss, in⸤ in spite of the criti⸤ and my assignme⸤ couraged, distrac⸤ halfway or three ⸤ to become all G⸤*

close to⸤
seeing ⸤
break is⸤
way. Th⸤
have to ⸤
come to⸤
too long.⸤
invested⸤

You ⸤
work in m⸤
it. So I'm ⸤
going to k⸤
going to k⸤
you do tha⸤
are one day⸤
ish line.

The Strength You Need

*As your days, so shall
your strength be.*

DEUTERONOMY 33:25 NKJV

The Scripture says your strength will always be equivalent to what you need. If you were to get a negative medical report, you're going to have the strength to deal with it. You're not going to fall apart.

When my father went to be with the Lord, my first thought was, *How am I going to deal with this?* My dad and I were very close. But rather than being devastated by his loss, I felt a peace I had never felt, a strength, a resolve. In my mind there were thoughts of worry and discouragement, but in my spirit I could hear God whispering, "Joel, I'm in control. It's all going to work out. I have you in the palm of My hand." That was finishing grace pushing me forward, propelling me into my destiny.

16

Strength in Reserve

God is our refuge and strength,
a very present help in trouble.

PSALM 46:1 NKJV

As long as you drive a large SUV with an eight-cylinder engine on flat roads, the engine is quiet. But when you start going up a steep mountain road, just when you think the vehicle won't make it, you hear those extra two cylinders kick in and actually feel the extra power. It is always available as strength in reserve.

The good news is that God has some strength in reserve for you. When you hit a tough time, don't worry. In the difficulties of life, if you will get quiet and turn off the negative voices, you will feel a peace that passes understanding. You're going to feel a force pushing you forward, taking you where you could not go on your own. You should be falling apart, but there is grace for every season.

Do Not Fear

"So do not fear, for I am with you; do not be dismayed, for I am your God. I will strengthen you and help you..."

ISAIAH 41:10

I've learned that the closer you get to your destiny, the tougher the battles become. The higher you go up the mountain, the more God promotes you. The critics will come out of the woodwork. People may not celebrate you. There will be unexpected challenges—a health issue, a business slows down, or you lose a loved one.

That challenge is a sign that you are close to your destiny. The same God who gave you the grace to start is the same God who is going to help you finish. Nothing you're facing is a surprise to Him. He knows every hill, every disappointment, and every setback. You're going to overcome obstacles that looked insurmountable, accomplish dreams that you thought were impossible. How can you do this? Finishing grace. You tap into strength in reserve.

Not Bound

...for which I am suffering, bound with chains as a criminal. But the word of God is not bound!

2 TIMOTHY 2:9 ESV

The Apostle Paul was sharing the good news and helping other people, but then he was arrested and put in prison. The closer he got to his destiny, the more obstacles he faced. He was alone in a dungeon. It looked as though God had forgotten about him. But Paul wasn't feeling sorry for himself. Even though he was in chains, they couldn't stop what God wanted him to do.

Since Paul couldn't go out and speak publicly, he thought, *No problem. I'll start writing.* He wrote nearly half of the books of the New Testament, much of it from a prison cell. They thought they were stopping him, but they caused his voice to become amplified. Some two thousand years later, and we still feel Paul's influence. What they meant for harm, God used for good.

More Grace

But he gives us more grace.
That is why Scripture says: "God opposes
the proud but shows favor to the humble."

JAMES 4:6

People may try to push you down, discredit you, belittle you, or leave you out. Don't get upset. Quit focusing on who is against you. They are a part of the plan to get you to your destiny. God will use them to propel you forward.

God has the final say. He brought Joseph out of prison. Paul stayed in prison, but they both fulfilled their destinies. If God doesn't turn it around the way you thought, right in the midst of those difficulties, you can shine, be a bright light, and have God's favor as Paul did. Bottom line is this: No person can stand against our God. No bad break can keep you from your destiny. God has given you finishing grace. He is going to get you to where you're supposed to be.

Finish with a Smile

This is the only race worth running.
I've run hard right to the finish,
believed all the way. All that's left
now is the shouting—God's applause!

2 TIMOTHY 4:7 MSG

When Paul came to the end of his life, he said, "I finished my course with joy." Notice, he didn't finish defeated, depressed, or sour. He finished with a smile on his face. He finished with a spring in his step. He finished with a song in his heart. That's what it means to have a flourishing finish.

We all have things come against us. You have to make up your mind, *I'm not only going to finish my course; I'm going to finish it with joy, with a good attitude. Not complaining, but with a song of praise. Not looking at what's wrong in my life, but thanking God for what's right in my life.* When you tap into finishing grace, you won't drag through your life. You will enjoy your life.

Guard Your Flame

*I remind you to fan into flame the gift
of God, which is in you through the
laying on of my hands.*

2 TIMOTHY 1:6

There was a famous race in ancient Greece called the Torch Race. The runners received a lit torch, and the goal was to reach the finish as fast as possible with the torch still burning. The runner had to keep the flame from wind or rain or anything that might put it out.

It's the same principle in the race of life. If you're going to finish your course with joy, you have to guard your flame. Too many people have lost their passion. They've lost their zeal. If that's you, there is a flame that is still alive on the inside of you. The Scripture talks about how we must fan the flame, stir up the gifts. It's not enough to just finish. You have to finish your course with your fire still burning.

Finish the Work

"My food," said Jesus,
"is to do the will of him who
sent me and to finish his work."

JOHN 4:34

For as long as I can remember, my father struggled with high blood pressure. Toward the end of his life, he didn't feel well, but he never missed a Sunday of preaching. He was determined to finish his course with joy.

One night he wasn't feeling well. He asked my brother-in-law Gary to come over and visit with him. Gary asked him what he thought about the difficulties he was having. My father said, "Gary, I don't understand it all, but I know this: His mercy endures forever." Those were the last words my father ever spoke. Right then, he breathed his final breath and went to be with the Lord. Even with his last words, he was magnifying his God. He crossed the finish line with his fire still burning, with his torch still lit.

Endure Till the End

The race is not to the swift or the battle to the strong...

ECCLESIASTES 9:11

During the marathon in the 1968 Olympic Games, a runner from Tanzania fell and broke his leg, but somehow he managed to continue running. Long after everyone else had finished the race, he struggled into the stadium. The few thousand remaining people saw him and began to cheer him on. Drawing strength from the crowd, he began to smile and wave as if he was going to win the gold medal. It was a moving moment later seen around the world.

The Scripture talks about how the race is not for the swift but for those who endure till the end. You don't have to finish first. You're not competing with anybody else. Just finish *your* course. Keep your fire burning. Dig your heels in and say, "I am determined to finish my course."

Be a Warrior

Join with me in suffering,
like a good soldier of Christ Jesus.

2 TIMOTHY 2:3

We all go through challenges, disappointments, and unfair situations. It's easy to let it overwhelm us to where we think, *This relationship issue is going to be the end of me. I can't deal with this illness or difficult child.*

God would not have allowed it if you couldn't handle it. But as long as you tell yourself it's too much, you'll talk yourself out of it. Have a new perspective. You are full of "can do" power. You are strong in the Lord. All through the day, whether you're stuck in traffic or facing a major disappointment, your attitude should be, *I can handle it. I can handle this grouchy boss. I can handle these people talking about me.* You can't have a weak, defeated mentality. You have to have a warrior mentality.

The Victory Given

*But thanks be to God! He gives us
the victory through our Lord Jesus Christ.*

1 CORINTHIANS 15:57

Joseph was sold into slavery by his brothers and spent years in a foreign prison for something that he didn't do. But his attitude was, *God is still on the throne. He wouldn't have allowed it unless He had a purpose for it. I will stay in faith and keep being my best.* In the end, he was made second in charge over all of Egypt.

My mother was diagnosed with terminal liver cancer in 1981 and given just a few weeks to live. She could have fallen apart and said, "God, it's not fair." Instead her attitude was, *I'm a victor. Nothing can snatch me out of God's hands.* Today, my mother is still going strong, healthy, full of joy, and helping others. No person, bad break, or sickness can keep you from your destiny.

Infused with Strength

I can do all things [which He has called me to do] through Him who strengthens and empowers me...

PHILIPPIANS 4:13 AMP

SEPTEMBER 26

The Apostle Paul said, "I am ready for anything. I am equal to anything through Him who infuses strength into me." He was stating, "The enemy may hit me with his best shot, but it won't stop me. I'm more than a conqueror."

Paul had been shipwrecked, spent the night on an open sea, and gone days without food. He was falsely accused, beaten with rods, and thrown into prison. If anyone had a reason to be negative and bitter, it would have been Paul. But his attitude was: *I can handle it. Almighty God, the Creator of the universe, has infused me with strength. He has equipped me, empowered me, anointed me, crowned me with favor, put royal blood in my veins, and called me to reign in life as a king.*

An Untroubled Heart

27

*"Do not let your hearts
be troubled. You believe in
God; believe also in me."*

JOHN 14:1

My father, back in the 1950s, was the
pastor of a large denominational
church, and his future looked very bright.
But through a series of events, he had to
leave that church. It was a major setback, a
big disappointment. But he didn't sit around
nursing his wounds. His attitude was, *I can
handle it. I know when one door closes, God
always opens up another door.* He and my
mother went out and launched Lakewood
Church, and here we are today still going
strong.

In difficult times, you have to talk to
yourself the right way. If you don't talk to
yourself, your thoughts will talk to you.
They will tell you, "It's too much. It's never
going to change. It's not fair. If God loved
you, He would have never let this happen."

Built on the Rock

"He makes His sun rise on the evil and on the good, and sends rain on the just and on the unjust."

MATTHEW 5:45 NKJV

Just because we're a person of faith doesn't exempt us from difficulties. Jesus told a parable about a person who built his house on a rock. He honored God. Another person built his house on the sand. He didn't honor God. The same storm came to both people. The wind blew and the rain fell on both houses. The difference is that when you honor God, the storm may come, but when it's all said and done, you will still be standing. The other house built on the sand was washed away. The enemy may hit you with his best shot, but because your house is built on the rock, his best will never be enough. You will come through the storm stronger, increased, promoted, and better than you were before.

Take Hold of Strength

"Or let him take hold of My strength, that he may make peace with Me; and he shall make peace with Me."

ISAIAH 27:5 NKJV

When you declare, "I can handle it," you're taking hold of strength. When you say it, you're getting stronger. That's why the Scripture says, "Let the weak *say,* 'I am strong.'" Listen to what you're saying to yourself. "I can't stand this job." "This class is too difficult." "My boss is the worst." If you're always talking about problems, that's draining you. When you talk defeat, strength and energy are leaving.

Quit letting those things overwhelm you. You are not a victim. You are a victor. If it came your way, you are ready for it and equal to it. If you will stay in agreement with God, He will take what is meant for your harm, and He will use it to your advantage. That difficulty won't defeat you. It will promote you.

It Will Promote You

*With God we will gain the victory,
and he will trample down our enemies.*

PSALM 108:13

I read about a businessman who had worked for a large home improvement company for over thirty years. He helped build that business from the ground up. But one day they decided they no longer needed him. Of course, he was disappointed, but he had the attitude, *This is not going to defeat me. It's going to promote me.*

In difficult times you have to remind yourself that nothing is a surprise to God. He's already written every day of your life in His book. If you'll stay in faith, your book ends in victory. This executive got a couple of his friends together, and they started their own company, "The Home Depot." What am I saying? That difficulty is not meant to defeat you. It's meant to promote you.

In the Furnace

*"See, I have refined you, though not as silver;
I have tested you in the furnace of affliction."*

ISAIAH 48:10

The fact is that God is not going to deliver us from every difficulty. He is not going to keep us from every challenge. If He did, we would never grow. When you're in a tough time, that's an opportunity to show God what you're made of. Anybody can get negative, bitter, and blame God. It's easy to lose your passion. But if you want to pass the test, if you want God to take you to a new level, you can't be a weakling. You have to be a warrior.

Dig your heels in and declare with Paul, "I can handle it. I'm ready for it. I'm equal to it. I know God is still on the throne. He is fighting my battles, and on the other side of this difficulty is a new level of my destiny."

Take the High Road

And whatever you do, whether in word or deed, do it all in the name of the Lord Jesus, giving thanks to God the Father through him.

COLOSSIANS 3:17

Maybe at the office you're not being treated fairly. It doesn't take any faith to go to work negative, discouraged, and complaining. If you want to pass the test, go to work with a positive attitude and do more than you're required. At your home, maybe your spouse is not treating you the way they should. It's easy to think, *I'm going to treat him the way he treats me.* If you want to pass the test, you have to be good to people even when they're not being good to you.

You have to do the right thing when the wrong thing is happening. See it as an opportunity to grow. Every time you do the right thing, a blessing will follow. When you take the high road, there will always be a reward.

Put on the New

*...and have put on the new self,
which is being renewed in knowledge
in the image of its Creator.*

COLOSSIANS 3:10

Too often a mistake we make is to tell ourselves, "It's not right. When they change, when it improves, then I'll have a better attitude." You have to make the first move. You do your part, and God will do His part. Quit worrying about God changing another person, and first allow God to change you.

Is there something you're letting overwhelm you? Why don't you get up every morning and make this simple declaration, "God, I want to thank You that I can handle anything that comes my way today. I can handle my plans not working out. Lord, thank You that I'll have a good attitude wherever I am." You have to decide before you leave the house that nothing that comes your way is going to upset you. Decide ahead of time.

A Quiet Spirit

If your boss is angry at you, don't quit! A quiet spirit can overcome even great mistakes.

ECCLESIASTES 10:4 NLT

So often in life we let what we feel is unfair to immediately upset us. We need to start believing we are empowered and ready for anything.

Friend, God is in complete control. You don't have to get upset when things don't go your way. You have the power to remain calm. You can handle any situation. Quit letting little things steal your joy. Every day is a gift from God. Life is too short to live it negative, offended, bitter, and discouraged. Start passing the tests. Start believing that God is directing your steps. Believe that He is in control of your life. Believe that He has solutions to problems that you haven't even had. If you will stay calm and stay in faith, God promised that all things will work out for your good.

It Won't Stick

*Now I know that the
LORD saves His anointed;
He will answer him from His
holy heaven with the saving
strength of His right hand.*

PSALM 20:6 NKJV

We've all seen how a spider spins a web that is filled with a sticky substance, so when another insect comes in contact with it, it actually gets stuck. So how does the spider that's spinning the sticky web walk across it and not get stuck? God made the spider so that its body releases a special oil that flows down to the legs. That way it can just slide across the web. You could say the spider doesn't get stuck because of the anointing that's on its life.

In a similar way, God has put an anointing on your life. It's like oil that causes things not to stick. When you walk in your anointing, knowing that you can handle anything that comes your way, things that should bring you down won't be able to.

Equipped and Empowered

I would have lost heart, unless I had believed that I would see the goodness of the LORD in the land of the living.

PSALM 27:13 NKJV

Perhaps you wonder how you made it through that slow season at work, through that illness, or through that breakup. It's because of the anointing God put on your life. He gave you strength when you didn't think you could go on. He gave you joy when you should have been discouraged. He made a way when it looked impossible.

Bottom line: God has infused strength into you. He has equipped and empowered you. You are ready for and equal to anything that comes your way. When you face difficulties, remind yourself, "I am anointed for this. I'm not going to fall apart. I'm not going to start complaining. I know God is still on the throne. He is fighting my battles, and if God be for me, who dare be against me?"

You Can Do It

"We should go up and take possession of the land, for we can certainly do it."

NUMBERS 13:30

A friend of mine has had cancer three times. I've never once heard him complain. He's got a warrior mentality. When the cancer came back for the third time, the doctors told him that before he took chemo they were going to harvest his white blood cells to help restore his immune system after the treatment. He asked the doctors how many of these cells they needed. They gave him a number. He said, "I'm going to give you twice what you need." For the next couple of months, all through the day he went around saying, "Father, thank You that my white blood cells are multiplying. They're getting stronger, increasing." He ended up giving four times the amount that they were hoping for. Today he is totally cancer-free, healthy, and strong.

Don't Be Intimidated

And in no way be alarmed or intimidated [in anything] by your opponents...

PHILIPPIANS 1:28 AMP

Don't be intimidated by that financial problem. Don't be intimidated by cancer. It's no match for you. Sickness cannot keep you from your destiny. God has you in the palm of His hand. Nothing can snatch you away. If it's not your time to go, you're not going to go. Don't be intimidated by what somebody said about you. There is an anointing on your life that seals you, protects you, enables you, and empowers you. God has infused you with strength. The Scripture calls it "can do" power.

There is a force in you that is more powerful than any opposition. Greater is He that is in you than anything that comes against you. When you have this warrior mentality, this "I can handle it" attitude, all the forces of darkness cannot keep you from your destiny.

Be Strong

*"Be strong and courageous.
Do not be afraid or terrified
because of them, for
the LORD your God goes
with you; he will never leave
you nor forsake you."*

DEUTERONOMY 31:6

When our children were young, we were at the beach one time when a bumblebee came and frightened my daughter. I swatted him out of the way, but thirty seconds later, he was right back. I grabbed my towel and knocked it down to the sand, but a minute later he was flying by our heads. This time I got my tennis shoe and squashed him into the sand as hard as I possibly could. To my amazement he got back up again and buzzed by my head at least three times. At that point I felt he deserved to live. He won.

That's the way you need to see yourself. No matter how big that enemy looks, just be like that bumblebee—refuse to fall into self-pity, refuse to let it overwhelm you, refuse to give up.

Better Than Ever

*It is God who arms
me with strength and
keeps my way secure.*

PSALM 18:32

Sometimes in life it feels as though we got blindsided. The relationship didn't make it. A business goes down. It may be a surprise to us, but it is not a surprise to God. Don't sit around nursing your wounds. Keep being your best. Keep honoring God. He has already given you the strength, the wisdom, the favor, and the determination not only to make it through, but to come out better than you were before.

Remember, you can handle it. Take hold of this strength. Remind yourself, "I'm ready for and equal to anything that comes my way. I am strong." If you will do this, God promises He will infuse strength into you. You will overcome every obstacle, defeat every enemy, and live the victorious life that belongs to you.

Divine Empowerment

"...how God anointed Jesus of Nazareth with the Holy Spirit and power, and how he went around doing good and healing all who were under the power of the devil..."

ACTS 10:38

We don't have to go through life doing everything on our own, trying to accomplish our dreams in our own ability, trying to overcome challenges in our own strength, our own intellect, and our own hard work. We have an advantage. God has placed His anointing on you. The anointing is a divine empowerment. It enables you to do what you could not do on your own. It will cause you to accomplish dreams even though you don't have the talent. It will help you overcome obstacles that looked insurmountable.

The anointing is only activated where there is faith. Instead of complaining about how it's not going to work out or how you'll never accomplish your dreams, turn that around and start declaring, "I am anointed. I am equipped. I am empowered. I am well able."

Fresh Oil

*But my horn [my emblem of strength and power]
You have exalted like that of a wild ox; I am
anointed with fresh oil [for Your service].*

PSALM 92:10 AMP

I've heard it said, "The anointing to us is like gasoline to a car." You can have the most expensive car, but if you don't put gasoline in it, you're not going anywhere. In a similar way, you've been made in the image of Almighty God. You are full of incredible potential. The fuel you need to release your greatness, to overcome obstacles, and to accomplish dreams is the anointing on your life.

He has already equipped and empowered you for every situation. When you are speaking words of victory, "I can do all things through Christ. I am strong in the Lord," you are putting fuel in your car. You're stirring up your anointing. That's when you'll go places that you couldn't go on your own. That's what keeps you moving forward.

Break Every Yoke

...his burden will be taken away from your shoulder, and his yoke from your neck, and the yoke will be destroyed because of the anointing oil.

ISAIAH 10:27 NKJV

Perhaps you're dealing with an illness. It hit you unexpectedly. You could let it overwhelm you and complain, "I can't believe this is happening to me." Instead, have a new perspective. That sickness is not a surprise to God. It didn't catch God off guard. He has already anointed you. You have the strength, the peace, the determination, and the confidence you need. You're anointed. The forces that are for you are greater than the forces that are against you. In those difficult times, you have to declare what Isaiah stated, "The anointing is breaking every yoke." "The anointing is greater than this depression." "The anointing is causing me to overcome." Every time you say, "I am anointed," chains are broken. Fear has to leave. Depression has to go. Healing comes. Strength comes. Faith comes.

Be Patient

So Samuel took the horn of oil and anointed him in the presence of his brothers, and from that day on the Spirit of the LORD came powerfully upon David.

1 SAMUEL 16:13

When David was a teenager, the prophet Samuel anointed him to be the next king of Israel. What's interesting is that after Samuel poured the anointing oil on his head, he sent David back to the fields to take care of the sheep. David lived as a shepherd for years even though he had a king's anointing.

As was true for David, even though you've been anointed, on the way to your destiny there will be times of testing, times of waiting where you have to be patient and keep doing the right things, where you don't see anything happening. You have to stay in faith and keep believing, *My time is coming. I may not see how it can happen, but I have a secret weapon. The anointing is on my life.*

A Royal Anointing

...much more will those who receive
the abundance of grace and the free
gift of righteousness reign in life
through the one man Jesus Christ.

ROMANS 5:17 ESV

The Scripture tells us that every one of us has a king's anointing, a queen's anointing. This means to live an abundant life, to accomplish your God-given dreams, to leave your mark on this generation.

You may think you don't have the skill, the talent, or the experience to accomplish what's in your heart, but that's okay. The anointing on your life will make up for what you don't have. You may have less talent, but with the anointing you will go further than people who have more talent. It is not just your intellect, your expertise, or your experience that determines how high you're going to go. It's the fact that Almighty God is breathing on your life. The anointing will cause you to accomplish dreams you could never accomplish on your own.

Not "Just" Anything!

"Villagers in Israel would not fight; they held back until I, Deborah, arose, until I arose, a mother in Israel."

JUDGES 5:7

In the book of Judges, one of the deliverers of Israel was Deborah, who describes herself as "a mother in Israel." This was significant. It was saying she didn't have an impressive position, title, influence, or prestige. She was a mother raising her children. Back in those days, women didn't have the leadership roles that they have today. Deborah would have been considered "just a mother."

But can I tell you that like Deborah, you're not "just" anything! You're a child of the Most High God. People may say, "You don't have the talent, the training, the position, or the intelligence." What they can't see is that God has put an anointing on you that supersedes all that, something that causes you to break barriers, to excel, to accomplish dreams, to do what you could not do.

It Was the Anointing

*"Wake up, wake up, Deborah!
Wake up, wake up,
break out in song!"*

JUDGES 5:12

The Scripture says that Israel had been held in the enemy's bondage for twenty years. It looked as if that's the way it would always be until Deborah, a mother in Israel, arose. God put a dream in Deborah's heart to do something about it. She could have said, "God, I'm just a mother raising my child. Nobody is going to listen to me. I don't have an army backing me up."

But Deborah understood this principle. She knew God had put something on her that would cause her to excel. Deborah took a step of faith, and other people began to join in. Before long the enemy's army was destroyed and order was restored. The nation was calm and peaceful. How could this mother affect the whole nation? It was the anointing on her life.

You Have an Anointing

But you have an anointing from the Holy One,
and all of you know the truth.

1 JOHN 2:20

I'm all for getting the best education you can, for developing your talents and improving your skills, but you are not limited to your own ability, your own education, your own intellect, or your own experience. Those will take you to a certain level, but to reach your highest potential you need the anointing on your life.

Quit making excuses as to what you can't do. "I'm just a mom." A mom with the anointing is more powerful than a CEO without it! "I'm just a student." "I'm just an accountant. I can't do anything great." Why not? Deborah, a mother, changed her whole nation. I can tell you firsthand, I'm not the most talented person. I don't have the most experience, the most training, or the most education, but I do have the anointing. So do you.

What It Takes

As for you, the anointing you received
from him remains in you...and as that
anointing is real, not counterfeit—
just as it has taught you, remain in him.

1 JOHN 2:27

When my father went to be with the Lord, I stepped up to pastor the church although I had never ministered before. Every voice told me, "You are not a minister. You're not going to know what to say. Nobody is going to listen to you." Instead of dwelling on those thoughts, I would look at myself in the mirror and say, "Joel, you are anointed. This is your moment. You've been raised up for such a time as this." I was stirring up the anointing.

There will always be negative voices that try to talk you out of your dreams, but let me encourage you. You're the man or woman for the job. You have what it takes. You're anointed. You're approved. You're talented enough. You're strong enough. You and God are a majority.

Live with Expectancy

*But I trust in you, LORD;
I say, "You are my God."
My times are in your hands...*

PSALM 31:14–15

OCTOBER
20

David spent years in the shepherds' fields, but he never forgot he had a king's anointing. It would have been easy for him to think, *Samuel anointed me, but he must have been wrong.* No, every day he kept reminding himself, "I am anointed. My time is coming. I will make a difference with my life."

God sees what you're doing and hears what you're saying. Every day you live in faith, with expectancy, you are one day closer to seeing your dreams come to pass. God knows when the right time is. If it hasn't happened yet, that means it's still on the way. God is getting you prepared. You're growing. You're getting stronger. What God has in your future is going to be greater than anything you've seen in the past.

Due Season

*And let us not grow
weary while doing good,
for in due season we shall
reap if we do not lose heart.*

GALATIANS 6:9 NKJV

Paul said your due season is coming. You're going to step into that king's anointing, that queen's anointing. You're just getting started. God's dream for your life is so much bigger than your own. If He would have done it earlier, you wouldn't have been prepared. Now is your time. You're about to step into what you were created to do. You're going to step into a new level of your destiny. The disappointments, the delays, and the setbacks in the past were all a part of the plan to get you prepared for right now. Nothing was wasted. It strengthened you. You developed trust, endurance, and confidence. Now you're prepared for this time. You're on the runway about to takeoff. You're going to see the exceeding greatness of God's favor!

Into the Palace

Then Saul sent messengers to Jesse and said, "Send me your son David, who is with the sheep."

1 SAMUEL 16:19

David was out in the shepherds' fields. It didn't look like anything was happening, but King Saul sent a message saying, "Send me David. I need him in the palace." David started working for Saul. That was another step on the way to his destiny. He wasn't on the throne yet, but at least he made it to the palace.

You may feel like you're with the sheep today, doing something that feels insignificant. You know you have more in you, but you've been in the background year after year. Don't get discouraged. Your time is coming. God is going to take you from the background to the foreground. You have a king's anointing. Victory is coming. Promotion is coming. What God has spoken over your life will come to pass.

Above and Beyond

"...to loose the chains of injustice and untie the cords of the yoke, to set the oppressed free and break every yoke..."

ISAIAH 58:6

A single mother told me about her long struggle to make ends meet, working two jobs, long hours. But she knew deep down she was made for more than just constantly struggling, not having enough, and being away from her children so much. She kept reminding herself that the anointing can break the yoke of poverty and lack.

One day she was invited to dinner by a couple that lived down the street from her whom she had only met once. That night they gave her the keys to a brand-new car. She was able to sell her car and pay off most of her debts so she didn't have to work so much. I learned later that she married an executive from a large company. God has blessed them exceedingly abundantly above and beyond.

Running Over

You honor me by anointing my head with oil.
My cup overflows with blessings.

PSALM 23:5 NLT

David said, "Because I am anointed, my cup runs over." When you walk in your anointing, knowing who you are and whose you are, at some point your cup will run over. You will see God pour out blessings that you cannot contain. Don't you dare settle with the sheep in the shepherds' fields. The palace is coming.

Friend, you were not created to barely get by, to take the leftovers, to live out in the shepherds' fields. You were created for victory, for abundance, for the palace. The same God who increased the single mother can increase you. The anointing on your life will cause people to be good to you. It will cause you to be at the right place at the right time, bringing favor, promotion, and increase.

Doors Will Open

So David went to Saul and began serving him.
Saul loved David very much,
and David became his armor bearer.

1 SAMUEL 16:21 NLT

David was in the palace playing the harp for King Saul. It had been a temporary position, but David was so good at what he did, King Saul created a new position for David. He became an armor bearer. If you will be your best right where you are and excel in what you do, the right doors will open for you. There may not be room for promotion at your work, but your gifts will make room for you. If there is not a position, God can cause them to create a new position. Maybe you are part time, believing for more work. You need to get ready. As David did, you're going to become full time. You've been faithful and didn't slack off. You're going to step into that king's anointing.

Fresh Anointings

Then the men of Judah came to Hebron, and there they anointed David king over the tribe of Judah.

2 SAMUEL 2:4

When King Saul was killed in a battle, it was David's time. He was thirty years old and about to take the throne. At this time, Israel was divided into two kingdoms—Judah and Israel. First, Judah anointed David to be their king. He served there seven and a half years, then he brought the two kingdoms together. When he was thirty-seven years old, the men of Israel joined the men of Judah, and they anointed David again to be the king over all of Israel.

What's interesting is that David was anointed as a teenager to become the king. He could have declined the subsequent anointings as unnecessary. But David understood the importance of having a fresh anointing. You can't win today's battles on yesterday's anointing. You need to have a fresh anointing.

The Key to Success

When all the elders of Israel had come to King David at Hebron,...they anointed David king over Israel.

2 SAMUEL 5:3

If David would have taken the throne without the fresh anointing, he wouldn't have had the success he had. When you humble yourself and say, "God, I can't do this on my own. I need Your help. God, I need a fresh anointing," you're showing your dependency on Him. When you acknowledge God in that way, He will give you wisdom beyond your years.

Whenever you start a new job or a new position or a new class, always ask for that fresh anointing. You're saying, "God, I'm ready for new opportunities, new abilities, new friendships, and new ideas." Maybe you're facing a challenge today—your health, your finances, a relationship. Instead of complaining about it, why don't you say, "God, give me a fresh anointing to overcome this challenge." It's the anointing that breaks the yoke.

Receive Power

*Be strong in the Lord [draw
your strength from Him and be
empowered through your union
with Him] and in the power of
His [boundless] might.*

EPHESIANS 6:10 AMP

Too often we are trying to do things in our own strength. It's a struggle. No promotion. No increase. The reason things get stale and we just endure our marriage, endure the job, and drag through the day is we're not stirring up the anointing.

I believe today God is releasing a fresh anointing in your life. You're going to see negative situations turn around. Chains of addictions and bad habits are being broken. Healing, promotion, and restoration are coming. You're going to step into the fullness of your destiny. Every morning remind yourself, "I am anointed. I am equipped. I am empowered." Remember to always ask for that fresh anointing. If you do this, I believe and declare, as David did, you will make it to your throne and step into the fullness of your destiny.

Set Times

*And so after waiting patiently,
Abraham received what
was promised.*

HEBREWS 6:15

In life we're always waiting for something—waiting for a dream to come to pass, waiting to meet the right person, waiting for a problem to turn around. When it's not happening as fast as we would like, it's easy to get frustrated. But you have to realize that the moment you prayed, God established a set time to bring the promise to pass for your healing, your promotion, and your breakthrough. It may be tomorrow, or next week, or five years from now.

But when you understand that the time has already been set, it takes all the pressure off. You won't live worried, wondering when this is ever going to happen. You'll relax and enjoy your life, knowing that the promise has already been scheduled by the Creator of the universe.

Be Willing to Wait

*"As soon as you began to pray,
a word went out, which I have come to tell you,
for you are highly esteemed."*

DANIEL 9:23

Maybe you have been praying about a situation for a long time and don't see anything happening. You could easily be discouraged. But what if God allowed you to see into the future, and you saw that on February 12 at 2:33 in the afternoon, you were going to meet the person of your dreams? You wouldn't be discouraged. You would be excited because you know the big day is coming.

Here's where it takes faith. God promises that there are set times in our future, but He doesn't tell us when they will be. Your set time may be tomorrow morning or two years from now. Are you willing to wait with a good attitude, knowing that they're on the way? God has a set time. Don't let negative thoughts talk you out of it.

———— ※ ————

You Have a Rest

Now we who have believed enter that rest...

HEBREWS 4:3

On January 8, 1986, at four o'clock in the afternoon, I walked into a jewelry store to buy a battery for my watch. Out walked the most beautiful girl I had ever seen. It was Victoria. I didn't tell her, but I thought, *This is my set time ordained by the Most High God.*

In the same way, there are set times in your future. You've prayed, believed, and stood in faith. The way you know you're really believing is that you have a rest. You're at peace. Let me assure you that you're going to come into set times of favor, a set time where a problem suddenly turns around, a set time where you meet the right person, a set time where a good break thrusts you years ahead. The answer is on the way.

The Appointed Time

For the vision is yet for an appointed time; but at the end it will speak, and it will not lie. Though it tarries, wait for it; because it will surely come...

HABAKKUK 2:3 NKJV

NOVEMBER

1

Habakkuk did not say "the appointed time might come." Not, "I hope so." God has already set the date. The appointed time has already been put on your calendar. One translation says, "It won't be one second late."

Sometimes we think, *My friends are getting ahead of me in life. My coworkers are being promoted, but I'm still stuck here.* Don't get discouraged. Sometimes God will take you from A to B to C, and then thrust you all the way down to S, T, U, V. What happened? You hit a set time that pushed you years ahead. Just run your race. Keep honoring God with your life. Our God is not a random God. He is a precise God. He has lined up solutions for you down to the very second.

Precision Timing

*In their hearts humans plan
their course, but the LORD
establishes their steps.*

PROVERBS 16:9

I know a lady in her early thirties who was believing to meet the right man, but she was starting to wonder if it was going to happen. One day she had a flat tire and pulled over on the side of the freeway. In a few seconds, another car pulled over. Out stepped a handsome young man who not only changed her tire, but he invited her to dinner. They ended up falling in love. A year and a half later, they got married.

Think about how precise God's timing is. The tire had to go flat and he had to leave his work at just the right time and be on the right road with just the right flow of traffic. That was a set time ordained by the Creator of the universe.

Perfectly Detailed

Wait for the LORD;
be strong and take heart
and wait for the LORD.

PSALM 27:14

You can trust God's timing. What you're praying about and what you're believing for are not going to be one second late. If it hasn't happened yet, it doesn't mean God is mad at you. It doesn't mean it's never going to work out. God has already established the time down to the split second. You don't have to worry or live frustrated. Stay in peace. God has you in the palm of His hand. Your steps are being directed by the Creator of the universe; not randomly, not vaguely. Down to the most finite, small detail.

When you understand this, it takes all the pressure off. You won't go around wondering when something is going to happen. Whether it's twenty minutes or twenty years, you know that what God promised He will bring to pass.

Trust His Timing

For there is a time and a way for everything, although man's trouble lies heavy on him.

ECCLESIASTES 8:6 ESV

A great prayer we should pray every day is, "God, give me the grace to accept Your timing." I'd love to tell you that if you stay in faith, if you believe, God will always answer your prayer within twenty-four hours, or at least within the first week. But we know that's not reality. God promises He will be true to His Word, but He never puts a timeframe on it. It would be a lot easier if God told us when we were going to get well, when we would meet the right person, or when our child would straighten up. But that wouldn't take any faith. It takes faith to say, "God, I don't know *when* You are going to do it, but I trust You enough to believe that You *will* do it."

November 5

The Big Picture

*"As the heavens are higher than the earth,
so are my ways higher than your ways
and my thoughts than your thoughts."*

ISAIAH 55:9

God can see the big picture for our lives. He knows what's up ahead. He knows what we're going to need, who we're going to need, and when they need to show up. If God did everything we ask on our timetable, it would limit us because sometimes what we're asking for is too small. Sometimes the person we think we can't live without isn't going to be good for us, so He closes the door. Sometimes the promotion we want so badly would keep us from a much bigger promotion that He has for us three years down the road.

God has the advantage of seeing it all. How many times have I looked back and said, "God, thank You for not answering that prayer." God knows what He is doing.

Faith and Patience

...to imitate those who through faith and patience inherit what has been promised.

HEBREWS 6:12

We live in a society that wants everything right now. We're being programmed for immediacy. Don't make me wait. It's easy to have faith. "God, I believe I'm going to accomplish my dreams. God, I believe I'm going to overcome this obstacle." We have the faith part down.

Let's make sure we get the patience part down as well. "God, I'm not only going to believe for big things, but I trust Your timing. I'm not going to get discouraged if it doesn't happen immediately. I'm not going to give up because it's taken a week, a month, or five years. I know the set time is already in my future, so I'm going to wait with faith and patience because I know that it's on the way."

What We Can't See

Jesus replied, "You do not realize now what I am doing, but later you will understand."

JOHN 13:7

When Victoria was pregnant with our son, Jonathan, the first few months were very exciting. But by the eight month, she was saying, "I'm so uncomfortable. I want to have this baby right now." But we know the child is still growing, developing. If God let her have the baby early, the child may not be healthy.

Sometimes we pray, "God, give me this promise now. I'm uncomfortable. These people aren't treating me right. Business is slow." What we can't see is that something is not ready. Maybe God is still working on another person who's going to be involved. Maybe another situation that's going to be a part of your destiny is not in place yet. Or maybe God is doing a work in you, developing your character, growing you stronger in that process.

In God's Hands

God did not lead them along...the shortest
route to the Promised Land. God said,
"If the people are faced with a battle, they
might change their minds..."

EXODUS 13:17 NLT

God could see the big picture for the Israelites. He knew that if He took them the shortest way, their enemies would be too powerful and they would be defeated. So on purpose, God took them a longer route to protect them and to strengthen them so that they could fulfill their destiny.

If something is not happening on your timetable, remind yourself, "God knows what He is doing. He has my best interests at heart. I wouldn't be having this delay unless God had a very good reason for it." And while you're waiting, don't make the mistake of trying to figure everything out. That's only going to frustrate you. Turn it over to God. Say with David, "God, my times are in Your hands. I'm not going to worry about why something hasn't happened."

God's Way

But Sarah saw that the son whom Hagar the Egyptian had borne to Abraham was mocking...

GENESIS 21:9

God gave Abraham and Sarah the promise that they were going to have a baby, but years went by and nothing was happening, so they tried to help God out. Sarah had Abraham sleep with one of her maids, and they had a baby whom they named Ishmael, but it wasn't the child God promised them and caused constant problems. Fourteen years later, at the set time, Sarah gave birth to Isaac, the child whom God promised them.

As was true for Sarah, there will be times in life where you'll be tempted to try to force things to happen. If you'll let go of Ishmael, Isaac will show up. The one God promised you is in your future. The time has already been set. Be patient and trust God to do it His way.

Don't Force Things

*Delight yourself also in the
LORD, and He shall give you
the desires of your heart.*

PSALM 37:4 NKJV

There's a big difference between God giving you the desires of your heart and you having to work to make it happen. When we try to force things, it's a constant struggle. It's a burden. But if you'll let God do it His way, in His timing, there'll be a grace. There will be an ease. Yes, you'll have opposition. But you'll feel a strength, a peace, God's favor pushing you forward.

I learned a long time ago that God doesn't need my help. You don't have to try to force doors to open. You don't have to try to make people like you or manipulate your way into a friendship or a position. Just keep honoring God with your life, stay in peace, trust His timing, and God will open doors that no man can shut.

Watch in Hope

But as for me, I watch in hope for the LORD,
I wait for God my Savior; my God will hear me.

MICAH 7:7

A couple of years after my father died, I had a strong desire to write a book, but I didn't know any publishers. Several times I started to call a friend who knew a publisher, but I didn't feel good about it. Over the next couple of years, I was approached by different publishers, but inside I could hear a still small voice telling me, "Joel, be patient. Something better is coming." I didn't worry about it.

One day through a series of unusual events, I met this publisher. I knew they were the right people. I felt good about it. Everything fell into place. And that book, *Your Best Life Now*, went on to become a huge success and has been published in many languages. That's what happens when you wait for God's timing. He will give you what He promised.

Your Heart's Desires

The LORD works out everything to its proper end...

PROVERBS 16:4

If you get a negative medical report, you lose your biggest client, or somebody is trying to make you look bad, it's easy to get all wrought up and think, *I have to get in there and straighten things out. I'm going to fix that person. I have to get a second job. I'll never make it without that client.*

You can do the right thing at the wrong time and miss God's best. Timing is everything. Be patient and let God open the doors. You may have to knock. You'll have to put forth the effort. I'm a believer in being aggressive and pursuing dreams, but you don't have to force doors to open. If you'll be patient and wait for God's timing, He will *give* you the desires of your heart.

Be Still and Know

He says, "Be still, and know that I am God..."

PSALM 46:10

When you feel overwhelmed and you're tempted to take everything into your own hands, you have to make yourself be still. This is when many people make quick decisions that end up only making matters worse. The battle is not yours. The battle is the Lord's. But as long as you're fighting it, trying to make it happen your way, God is going to step back and let you do it on your own. But when you take it out of your hands and say, "God, I trust You. I know You have already set the time to bring me out. You've already set the time to vindicate me. You've set the time to bring healing. So I'm going to be still and know that You are God," that's when God will fight your battles.

Show His Power

*"You need not fight
in this battle; take your
positions, stand and witness
the salvation of the LORD
who is with you..."*

2 CHRONICLES 20:17 AMP

The Israelites were surrounded by a huge army and greatly outnumbered. They were so worried and stressed out. Just before they went to battle, they decided to pray. Notice the condition. If you will be still and remain at rest, God will turn it around. God will restore you. God will vindicate you.

Maybe you're facing a big challenge. You're upset and frustrated. God is saying to you what He said to them, "Be still. I've already set the time to not only bring you out, but to bring you out better off than you were before." Now do your part and rest. We may not understand why something is taking so long, but sometimes God will delay an answer on purpose simply so He can show His power in a greater way.

Long Ago Ordained

*"Have you not heard?
Long ago I ordained it.
In days of old I planned it;
now I have brought it to pass..."*

ISAIAH 37:26

Your situation may be taking longer than you thought. Maybe it's something more difficult than you've ever experienced. It doesn't mean that God went on vacation and is not concerned anymore. God has not turned it around yet because He wants to show His favor in your life in an amazing way. God is going to show His strength, His healing, His goodness, and His power like you've never seen before. You might as well get ready. When God brings you out, everybody around you is going to have no doubt that the God you serve is an awesome God.

Because you have faith and patience, I believe and declare, you're going to come into set times of favor. God is going to give you the desires of your heart.

While We Were Sinners

But God demonstrates his own love for us in this: While we were still sinners, Christ died for us.

ROMANS 5:8

Most of the time we believe God loves us as long as we're making good decisions, resisting temptation, and treating people right. We know God is on our side. But there will be times when you compromise, times when you have doubts, times when you fail. When we don't perform perfectly, it's easy to think that God is far from us.

I say this respectfully, but sometimes religion pushes people down. It says, "If you turn your back on God, He will turn His back on you. If you make poor choices, you're on your own." But the truth is that when you fall, God doesn't turn away from you. He comes running toward you. When you blow it, God doesn't say, "Too bad. You had your chance." He comes after you with a greater passion.

Imperfect People

*"While he was still a long way off,
his father saw him and was filled with
compassion for him; he ran to his son,
threw his arms around him and kissed him."*

LUKE 15:20

When you make a mistake, God loves you so much that He pursues you. He won't leave you alone until He sees you restored and back on the right course. He will express His love in a greater way. He will send people across your path to encourage you, to help reignite your faith. That's the mercy of God coming after you, saying, "You may have blown it, but you're still My child. You may have let Me down, but I'm not going to let you down. You may have lost faith in Me, but I haven't lost faith in you."

We don't have to have a perfect performance where we never have a doubt or make a mistake. Certainly, we should try our best each day to honor God. But God loves imperfect people.

His Amazing Love

Then Peter remembered the word Jesus had spoken: "Before the rooster crows, you will disown me three times." And he went outside and wept bitterly.

MATTHEW 26:75

Before Jesus chose Peter to become a disciple, Jesus knew that Peter would deny Him, but He chose him anyway. God knows every mistake that we will ever make. You can imagine how Peter must have felt when he denied knowing Jesus during His trial. When Jesus needed him the most, if He ever needed a friend to stick up for Him, it would have been right then, but Peter didn't do it. No doubt he was beating himself up with guilt for betraying Jesus.

The good news is, God still chose Peter, and He still chooses us. He still says, "That's My child," and He will still help you fulfill your destiny as He did Peter. Why? Because God's love is not based on our performance. It's based on our relationship. We are His children.

God Comes after You

"But go, tell his disciples and Peter, 'He is going ahead of you into Galilee. There you will see him, just as he told you.'"

MARK 16:7

We've all made mistakes. But none of us have failed as big as Peter in his betrayal of Jesus. You would think that Peter would have missed his destiny. Surely God wouldn't have anything to do with him. No, when you fail, God doesn't love you less. He comes after you.

They crucified Jesus on Friday. On Sunday morning, an angel appeared and told Mary Magdalene, "Jesus is risen. Now go tell His disciples and Peter that He is alive." Out of all the disciples whom God could have mentioned at this historic time, the only person He specifically pointed out was Peter. God was saying, "Peter, I know you think I'll never have anything to do with you. But Peter, when you turn your back on Me, I don't turn My back on you."

Receive God's Mercy

There is therefore now no condemnation to those who are in Christ Jesus, who do not walk according to the flesh, but according to the Spirit.

ROMANS 8:1 NKJV

After his betrayal of Jesus, Peter could have gotten stuck in condemnation and guilt. I can imagine that when he heard Mary say, "Peter, the angel specifically said to tell you that Jesus is alive," something ignited on the inside. He shook off the guilt, shook off the self-pity, and said, "I may have blown it in the past, but that doesn't have to keep me from my future. I'm still going to become who God has created me to be."

God is saying to all the people who have fallen, the people who have made mistakes, "I still love you. I still believe in you. If you will let go of the guilt and move forward, I will still get you to where you are supposed to be." Do your part and receive God's mercy.

Restoration

Those who believed what Peter said were baptized and added to the church that day—about 3,000 in all.

ACTS 2:41 NLT

Not long after Peter was forgiven and restored after his betrayal of Jesus, he went out and ministered, and three thousand people came to know the Lord—the most ever recorded in the Scripture. God doesn't write us off when we make mistakes. God doesn't cancel our destiny because we've taken a few detours.

Maybe today, you're down on yourself because you're not where you thought you would be in life. You've made some poor choices. Now you're letting the guilt weigh you down. That heaviness is keeping you from God's best. God is calling your name today, saying, "I have forgiven you. I am not disappointed in you or withholding My blessing. I still have an amazing future in front of you." He is running toward you.

The God of Jacob

Then he said, "I am the God of your father, the God of Abraham, the God of Isaac and the God of Jacob."

EXODUS 3:6

In the Scripture, it talks about the God of Abraham, the God of Isaac, and the God of Jacob. I can understand how He is the God of Abraham, the father of our faith. I can understand how He is the God of Isaac, who was extremely obedient, even willing to be sacrificed. But when it says He is the God of Jacob, that doesn't make a lot of sense. Jacob was a cheater. He went around deceiving people. He stole his brother's birthright. Jacob was known for making poor choices.

What was God saying? "I'm not just the God of perfect people. I'm not just the God of people who never make a mistake. I'm the God of people who have failed. I'm the God of people who have blown it."

He Is Your God

Then the man said, "Your name will no longer be Jacob, but Israel, because you have struggled with God and with humans and have overcome."

GENESIS 32:28

It's interesting that later in Jacob's life, when he got his life straightened out, God changed his name from Jacob to Israel. That was to signify his new beginning. God could have been known as the God of Abraham, Isaac, and Israel. That was Jacob's new redeemed name. But God on purpose left it as the God of Abraham, Isaac, and Jacob to forever settle it that "I'm not just the God of perfect people. I'm the God of imperfect people, too."

You may have made mistakes, but be encouraged. He is the God of Jacob. He is still your God. You may have lost your temper, struggled with an addiction, or compromised your integrity. Don't beat yourself up. He is the God of Jacob. He is your God, too.

Jesus the Messiah

Then Jesus declared,
"I, the one speaking to you—I am he."

JOHN 4:26

John 4 records the story of Jesus meeting a lady who has become known as "The Woman at the Well." She had been married five times and was living with a sixth man. You can imagine her heartache and pain. I'm sure she felt beaten down by life—not really living, just existing. It says Jesus "had to go through Samaria," even though there was a shorter route to His destination. He purposefully went to express His love for her.

It's interesting that the first person Jesus revealed Himself to as the Messiah was not the religious leaders. It was not the priests and the rabbis in the synagogue. It was this woman; a woman who had made mistakes, a woman who was beaten down by life—an imperfect person. That one encounter changed her life.

Get Back in the Game

*Let us then approach
God's throne of grace with
confidence, so that we may
receive mercy and find grace
to help us in our time of need.*

HEBREWS 4:16

Too many people, like "The Woman at the Well," are sitting on the sidelines of life. They feel as though they've blown it too many times. Now they're letting the accusing voices convince them that they're all washed up. "God is disappointed with you. You can't expect His favor."

You have to get this truth down into your spirit. You may have made mistakes, but God is running to you. He doesn't love you less. He loves you more. Quit thinking about what could have or should have been, and get back in the game. You're not supposed to sit on the sidelines. God is not disappointed in you. Do your part and start moving forward. You can still fulfill your destiny. God's mercy is bigger than any mistake that you've made.

A Perfect Heart

*For the eyes of the
LORD run to and fro
throughout the whole earth,
to shew himself strong in
the behalf of them whose
heart is perfect toward him.*

2 CHRONICLES 16:9 KJV

The Scripture doesn't say that God is
looking for a perfect performance. God
is looking for people who have a heart that
is turned perfect toward Him. That means
you get up each day with a desire to please
and honor God. But you will have times
when you fail to resist temptation. The good
news is that does not cancel your destiny.
Your performance may not be perfect, but
because your heart is perfect toward God,
He still has something amazing in your
future.

You can't change the past. Learn from
your mistakes, but don't get stuck there.
Receive God's mercy. Be bold enough to
say, "God, I blew it. I know I was wrong. But
God, I know You are not holding it against
me. I know You are the God of imperfect
people."

When You Doubt

"Put your finger here; see my hands. Reach out your hand and put it into my side. Stop doubting and believe."

JOHN 20:27

After Jesus had risen from the grave, everyone was so excited—except Thomas. He had spent just as much time with Jesus as the other disciples, yet they were full of faith. Thomas was full of doubt and questions. One day they were in a room together, and Jesus came walking *through* the doors and went straight to Thomas. He didn't say, "Thomas, what's wrong with you?" He said, "I understand. That's why I came to you first. Now feel the nail prints in My hands."

Notice the pattern. When you have doubts as Thomas did, when you blow it as Peter did, when you fail as the woman who was married five times did, we think God is so far away from us. It's just the opposite. God came to the people who had doubt before He came to the people who had faith.

Failure Is an Event

*But you were washed, you were
sanctified, you were justified in
the name of the Lord Jesus and
by the Spirit of our God.*

1 CORINTHIANS 6:11

Thomas doubted this one time, yet people have labeled him as "Doubting Thomas." The good news is God doesn't judge us by one mistake. Do you know what God calls him? Believing Thomas, Forgiven Thomas, Restored Thomas, Amazing Thomas. Thomas went on to become the one who brought the Good News to the nation of India.

Too often we get our performance mixed up with our identity. You may have failed, but you are not a failure. That's what you did. Failure is an event. That's not who you are. You are a child of the Most High God. You've been handpicked by the Creator of the universe. You may struggle with an addiction, but you are not an addict. That's what you did. That's not who you are. You are free. You are clean. You are restored.

No Condemnation

*...and through Him everyone who believes
[who acknowledges Jesus as Lord and Savior
and follows Him] is justified and declared
free of guilt from all things.*

ACTS 13:39 AMP

In life, we're all going to have times where we fall, makes mistakes, and blow it. I can assure you they will come up on the movie screen of your mind again and again. You have to get good at changing the channel. Quit replaying all the times that you've failed, the times you gave into temptation, the time you blew the relationship, the time it didn't work out. All that's going to do is depress you.

You will not be free from guilt or enjoy your life if you are constantly replaying the negative memories of your past. If you're going to replay anything, replay your victories. Put on your accomplishments. Put on your victories. Replay the time that you honored God. Replay the times that you helped someone else in need. That will change your perspective.

Walk in the Light

But if we walk in the light, as he is in the light, we have fellowship with one another, and the blood of Jesus, his Son, purifies us from all sin.

1 JOHN 1:7

Friend, your sins have already been forgiven. Every mistake you've made and ever will make has already been paid in full. The real question is, will you receive God's mercy? You don't have to go around feeling guilty, not excited about your future. God is running toward you today. He is saying, "You may have blown it. You may have failed. But I'm not disappointed in you. I still love you. I still believe in you. I still have an amazing future in front of you."

Your performance may not have been perfect, but because your heart is perfect toward Him, God is going to show Himself strong in your behalf. If you'll shake off the guilt and receive God's mercy, you will not only live freer but you will still become all you were created to be.

A Destiny Frame

By faith we understand that the worlds were framed by the word of God, so that the things which are seen were not made of things which are visible.

HEBREWS 11:3 NKJV

When the Scripture says "the worlds were framed by the Word of God," it's not just talking about the physical *worlds*. The word in the original language is *eons*, meaning, "ages" or "times." God has a frame around your times. He has put a fence, a boundary, around your life. Nothing can penetrate your frame that God doesn't allow. Trouble, sickness, accidents—they can't just randomly happen. The frame is set.

This is a destiny frame set by the Creator of the universe. Not only can nothing get in without God's permission, but you can't make a mistake big enough to break out of that frame. You may come right up to the edge and be about to do something to get you in trouble, but you'll bump into the frame. God will push you right back.

God's Protection

*A fool vents all his feelings,
but a wise man holds them back.*

PROVERBS 29:11 NKJV

A man told me how he had been so fed up with his boss's condescending ways that he was going to give the boss a piece of his mind, knowing he'd get fired. As he lay in bed the night before, he had his speech all lined up and was steaming over every word. The first thing the next morning, he marched into his boss's office without knocking. Then the strangest thing happened. He couldn't remember what he was going to say. He looked at the boss and said, "Uh...uh...would you like a cup of coffee?" He went completely blank.

What happened? He bumped into the frame. God knows how to protect you, not only from accidents, not only from the wrong people. God will protect you from yourself. Sometimes we're the most dangerous thing we face.

That's the Frame

Everyone should be quick to listen, slow to speak and slow to become angry, because human anger does not produce the righteousness that God desires.

JAMES 1:19–20

A person cuts you off on the freeway, and you're about to give them a signal with your hand. But when you pull up next to them so aggravated, instead of doing what you thought, you just smile and give them a friendly wave.

What happened? You bumped into your frame. This frame has kept you out of more trouble than you realize. You'd better thank God for your frame or you might not still have a job. If it had not been for the frame, we might not still be married. How many times were we going to tell our spouse exactly what we thought, and exactly what they should do, and we hear the still small voice saying, "Don't do it. Bite your tongue. Walk away." We take the advice. That's the frame.

Right to the Edge

"Praise be to the LORD, who...has kept his servant from doing wrong..."

1 SAMUEL 25:39

In the story recorded in 1 Samuel 25, after David and his men had protected a wicked rich man by the name of Nabal who had thousands of sheep, David was furious at the extreme disrespect Nabal showed to him. God sent Abigail, who was Nabal's wife, to intercept David before he struck with vengeance. She convinced David his actions could ruin his destiny.

You know what Abigail was? She was a part of the frame. God ordained her to be there at the right time, to know exactly the right thing to say. Had David gotten distracted, killed Nabal and all his men, caused a big stir by shedding innocent blood, that mistake could have kept him from taking the throne. David went right up to the edge, but he bumped into his frame.

Framed In

Now the LORD provided a huge fish to
swallow Jonah, and Jonah was in the belly
of the fish three days and three nights.

JONAH 1:17

Jonah experienced the frame. God told him to go to the city of Nineveh, but he refused and went in the opposite direction. God will always let you go your own way, but He is so merciful—at some point, you're going to bump into your frame. Jonah went in the wrong direction and ended up being thrown overboard and being swallowed by a huge fish.

Jonah didn't realize God had put a frame around his life. Yes, he made a mistake, but it wasn't outside the frame. God allowed the difficulty into Jonah's frame not to harm him but to push him toward his divine destiny. That fish was part of Jonah's frame. Three days later that fish spit him onto dry ground. Jonah said, "You know what? I think I'll go to Nineveh after all."

Strong Boundaries

If I rise on the wings of the dawn, if I settle on the far side of the sea, even there your hand will guide me, your right hand will hold me fast.

PSALM 139:9–10

As Jonah did, you can run as much as you want, but the good news is you'll never run out of your frame. You'll keep bumping up against it again and again. It will always push you back toward your divine destiny.

God has put a frame that you can't penetrate. The enemy can't penetrate. Drugs can't penetrate. The wrong people can't penetrate. The Most High God has fenced you in. He has put boundaries around your life so strong that all the forces of darkness cannot get in and you cannot get out. And yes, we can make mistakes. We can run from the call. We can try to ignore it. But the frame around your life was put in place before the foundation of time. When God breathed His life into you, He framed your world.

For Your Children

"The promise is for you and your children and for all who are far off—for all whom the Lord our God will call."

ACTS 2:39

Parents, God has the right people not only lined up for you, but for your children, for your grandchildren. They've been framed. They may get off course, but sooner or later they'll bump into the frame. They may run with the wrong crowd, but the frame is up. They can't go too far to miss their destiny. They're going to bump into it again, again, and again, until they finally say, "I'm tired of fighting. God, have Your way in my life."

Quit worrying about them and start thanking God for the frame. Get in agreement with God and say, "Lord, I want to thank You that my children have been framed. I've committed them into Your hands. And Lord, You said the seed of the righteous will be mighty in the land."

Prayer Power

I thank God, whom I serve, as my ancestors did, with a clear conscience, as night and day I constantly remember you in my prayers.

2 TIMOTHY 1:3

I know a mother who was so concerned about her son. He was running with the wrong crowd and ended up in jail. One Sunday morning he was arguing with another inmate about what to watch on the television when a huge inmate, who looked like a professional football player, grabbed the remote control and said to him, "We're going to watch Joel today, and you're going to watch with me." What happened? He bumped into the frame. As her son was watching the program, he began to feel God's presence. He started weeping. Right there in the jail that big inmate led him to Christ.

You may not see how it can happen. That's not your job. Your job is to stay in peace, knowing that your children have been framed. Your prayers are activating God's power.

Even When We...

Then the LORD opened the donkey's mouth, and it said to Balaam, "What have I done to you to make you beat me these three times?"

NUMBERS 22:28

When I was nineteen years old, I was driving home very late at night. There was almost nobody on the freeway. I thought, *I wonder how fast this car can go?* So I put the pedal to the floor and was flying down the highway when I noticed there was a car right next to me. I thought, *He wants to race.* So I pushed the gas pedal down even farther. When I looked over, this time he was holding up his badge. My heart stopped. I drove thirty miles an hour the rest of the way home.

Even when we do dumb things, we can't get out of the frame. God will always have the right person, even an off duty police officer at one in the morning, or a donkey to keep us in the frame.

Kicking
Doesn't Work

And the Lord said,
I am Jesus whom thou
persecutest: it is hard for thee
to kick against the pricks.

ACTS 9:5 KJV

In the Scripture, there was a man named Saul who was having believers put in prison, doing more harm to God's people than any other person of that time. One day a light so bright shone down on him that he fell to the ground and became blind. Then God said in effect, "Saul, I have you in My frame. You're trying to kick, trying to run, trying to ignore it, but the frame is not going to move. I have a destiny for you to fulfill, and it's not to stop My work. It's to advance My work." The voice told Saul to go to the city and see Ananias, who prayed for Saul. He got his sight back. Saul became the Apostle Paul, who went on to write almost half of the books of the New Testament.

His Call Is Irrevocable

...for God's gifts and his call are irrevocable.

ROMANS 11:29

The Creator of the universe has put a frame around your life. You can kick, run, and try to ignore it. That's just going to make you more miserable. It's hard to keep kicking against the calling on your life, the destiny you have to fulfill. God is not going to remove the frame.

It's wise if you just surrender and say, "God, my life is in Your hands. I'm going to live for You. I'm going to get rid of these friends who are pulling me down. I'm going to get help for these bad habits. I'm going to get in church and serve and grow. I'm going to pursue the dreams You have placed in my heart." The sooner you do that, the happier and the more fulfilling your life will be.

December 12

Permission Required

A thousand may fall at your side,
ten thousand at your right hand,
but it will not come near you.

PSALM 91:7

A part of this frame is a hedge of protection around your life that the enemy cannot cross. A friend of mine was driving home and stopped at a light. When it changed to green, he looked both ways. Then something said to him so strongly, "Look again!" A car was coming full speed, never attempted to stop, and ran right through the red light. If he had not looked a second time, he would have been broadsided.

What was that? The frame. If it's not your time to go, the enemy cannot take you out. The frame that's placed around your life was put there by the Most High God. That's why the psalmist said, "I'm not worried. It can't come near me. I know there's a frame around my life. Nothing can happen without God's permission."

Sheltered

For in the day of trouble he will keep me safe in his dwelling; he will hide me in the shelter of his sacred tent and set me high upon a rock.

PSALM 27:5

I had somebody complain to me once about how their brand-new car had been hit on the freeway and totaled. They didn't know if the insurance was going to cover it. They were upset and discouraged. They said, "If I have this frame, how come I had an accident?"

Keep the right perspective. You may have lost your car, but because of the frame, you didn't lose your life. I'm convinced that God protects us from so many things that we don't even realize. You can always thank God for what didn't happen. Because of the frame, you didn't have an accident. Because of the frame, you're not in the hospital. Because of the frame, you didn't get laid off. Because of the frame, your children are still healthy and whole.

Put There by God

"I will fulfill the number of your days."

EXODUS 23:26 NKJV

When I was at the Brooke Army Medical Center, a couple asked me to pray for their son who had been badly burned when he was a soldier in Iraq. In the middle of the night, he had been refueling large tanks of gas when something caused the tanks to ignite. When he woke up, he was flat on his back, on fire, unable to move. Out of nowhere two Iraqi civilian men showed up, started rolling him in the dirt, and stopped the fire. What's amazing is that those men were not allowed on the secured base. The parents said, "Those men were put there by God to save our son." What was that? The frame. It wasn't his time to go. God is bigger than an explosion, bigger than an accident. God has you in a frame.

Not Even Death

"I am the Living One; I was dead, and now look, I am alive for ever and ever! And I hold the keys of death and Hades."

REVELATION 1:18

When I was ten years old, our family went to Hawaii. We were so excited, and all five of us children ran down to the beach to play in the big waves. But in the excitement, we looked up and couldn't find my eight-year-old sister, April. We searched so frantically. We were sure April had drowned. An hour and fifteen minutes later, she was found alive and well. She had fallen asleep on her float and drifted nearly two miles down the shore. God had her in a frame.

Death can't penetrate your frame. God has to allow it. I always tell people who have lost a loved one, especially if they went home at an early age, the enemy doesn't have the power to take our loved ones. God calls them home. God receives them into His presence.

A Hedge of Protection

"Have you not put a hedge around him and his household and everything he has?"

JOB 1:10

Satan was looking for somebody to test. God said to Satan, "Have you seen my servant, Job? There's none like him in all the land." Satan answered back something interesting. He said, "Yes, but You know I can't touch him. You've got a frame around his life."

What I want you to see is the enemy can't just do whatever he wants. He has to ask God for permission. God has to allow him to do it. Job went through a time of testing. He fought the good fight. And in the end, not only did he not curse God, but he came out with double. When you go through tough times, don't get discouraged. Remember, the frame is still up. You keep moving forward, and God will bring you out better off than you were before.

※

Nothing Can Separate

*...neither death nor life,...neither the
present nor the future, nor any powers...
will be able to separate us from the love of
God that is in Christ Jesus our Lord.*

ROMANS 8:38–39

Don't worry about your future. You've been framed. There are boundaries around your life put in place by the most powerful force in the universe. Not only can nothing get in without God's permission, you can't get out. Now all through the day, instead of being stressed out, under your breath, say, "Lord, thank You that my life has been framed. Thank You that my children, my health, my finances, my dreams, and my future are in Your frame. I am protected."

If you'll do that, you'll not only be happier, you'll not only have more peace, but God promises the number of your days He will fulfill. You will see His protection, His mercy, and His favor. And nothing will keep you from your God-given destiny.

Share Your Life

Because we loved you so much, we were delighted to share with you not only the gospel of God but our lives as well.

1 THESSALONIANS 2:8

Many people are praying for a miracle. "God, please send me a friend. God, I need help with these children. I need training. God, I need a good break." We have to realize that we can become the miracle they need. God uses our lives to touch and encourage and bless others. God will bring people across our path so that we can be the answer to their prayers.

Take time to become the miracle. Be aware of who is in your life. God put them there on purpose. It's because you are full of miracles. There is healing in you. There is restoration, there's friendship, there are new beginnings. You can lift the fallen. You can restore the broken. You can be kind to a stranger. You can become someone's miracle.

Become a Miracle

"Greater love has no one than this: to lay down one's life for one's friends."

JOHN 15:13

My brother, Paul, is a surgeon and spends time in Africa operating on needy people in remote villages. One of the clinics is just a small tin building that barely has electricity, minimal medical supplies, and one doctor. A man came into the clinic who had been gored by an elephant tusk, right through his midsection. Paul took him back to the makeshift operating room to hopefully spare his life, but there was no blood supply with which to replenish the man. Before Paul operated, he took thirty minutes and gave his own blood. He operated on the young man, then replenished the blood the man had lost with his own blood. What was he doing? Becoming a miracle. He could have prayed, "God, he's in bad shape. He needs a miracle." Paul realized, *I am his miracle.*

Be the Answer

*...through love serve and seek
the best for one another.*

GALATIANS 5:13 AMP

What I want us to see is that God has put miracles in us. We can be the answer to someone's prayers. You can be the good break and help they're looking for. It may be teaching your coworker the skills you know. Or helping that family that's struggling with the rent. Or taking that young man to baseball practice with your son each week. It's no big deal to you, but it's a miracle to them. It's what will push them toward their destiny.

If we all had the attitude, *I am a miracle waiting to happen*, what kind of world would this be? Look around at who's in your life. Listen to what they're saying. Is there any way that you can help? Those are opportunities to become their miracle.

Offer Authentic Devotion

Be devoted to one another with [authentic] brotherly affection [as members of one family], give preference to one another in honor...

ROMANS 12:10 AMP

A good friend of mine grew up in the projects, very poor. His dream was to become a television journalist. Against all odds, he got a scholarship to a mostly white Ivy League university. He's African American. His roommate, who came from a very prestigious family, said, "If you're going to be a journalist, you have to increase your vocabulary." For four straight years, every day, this roommate had him use one new word in sentences all through the day.

What was this roommate doing? Becoming a miracle. He took the time to care. He realized his friend was in his life for a reason. Today, this young man is one of the top newscasters in America. But I wonder where he would be if his roommate had not taken the time to become a miracle.

Refresh Others

*A generous person will prosper;
whoever refreshes others
will be refreshed.*

PROVERBS 11:25

You may feel that you're the one who needs a miracle. Here's the key. If you will become a miracle, God will always make sure that you have the miracles that you need. As long as you're sowing these seeds, the right people, the right opportunities, and the breaks you need will be in your future. If you want your dream to come to pass, help somebody else's dream come to pass.

You can't help everyone, but you can help someone. There are people whom God has put in your path who are connected to your destiny. As you help them rise higher, you will rise higher. As you meet their needs, God will meet your needs. Reaching your highest potential is dependent on you helping someone else reach their potential.

Say "I Can"

Dear friends, let us love one another,
for love comes from God. Everyone who loves
has been born of God and knows God.

1 JOHN 4:7

I met two ladies whom I thought were mother and daughter. But the older lady said, "No, we're not, but she's just like my daughter." She told how before we moved our church to our new facility, she was telling a group of friends her concerns about whether she would be able to continue to come because she was uncomfortable driving the freeways. This young lady, whom she had never met before, overheard her, stepped up, and said, "I can bring you." The lady said, "Are you serious? Where do you live?" They lived thirty-minutes apart. But this young lady saw this as an opportunity to become a miracle. Now every Sunday morning, like clockwork, she brings the older lady to church. After the older lady told me the story, she hugged the young lady and said, "Joel, she's my miracle."

Which One Are You?

"He went to him and bandaged his wounds, pouring on oil and wine. Then he put the man on his own donkey, brought him to an inn and took care of him."

LUKE 10:34

Jesus told a parable about a man who had been beaten and left on the ground, almost dead. In a little while, first a priest and then a Levite (an assistant to the priests) came by but kept on going. Then a third man, a Samaritan, came by. Like the first two, he thought, *He sure needs a miracle.* But he said, "God put him in my path so I can be a healer, so I can be a restorer, so I can give him a new beginning," and he did so.

Which one are you? Helping others can be the key to seeing your situation turn around. The people you see who need encouragement, who need a ride, who need help accomplishing a dream—they are opportunities for you to go to a higher level.

The Heart of God

Religion that God our Father accepts as pure and faultless is this: to look after orphans and widows in their distress...

JAMES 1:27

In the parable we read about yesterday, the priest didn't have time to bother with the injured man. He had his religious duties to fulfill at the temple. After all, if he helped the man, he might get his white robe "unclean." He had all kinds of excuses. But true religion gets dirty. True religion doesn't hide behind stained glass or fancy clothes. It goes to where the needs are.

When you get down low to lift somebody up, in God's eyes, you can't get any higher. The closest thing to the heart of God is helping hurting people. When you take time to restore the broken, encourage them, wipe away their tears, let them know that there are new beginnings—that's the religion Jesus talked about. True religion doesn't judge people to see if they deserve our help.

Full of Miracles

On hearing this, Jesus said,
"It is not the healthy who need
a doctor, but the sick."

MATTHEW 9:12

God didn't call us to judge people; He called us to heal people. He called us to restore people. He called us to become their miracles. Anybody can find fault. Anybody can be critical and come up with excuses to pass on by those in need. That's easy. But where are the people who will take the time to care? Where are the people who will get down and dirty and help love them back into wholeness?

Don't be a passerby who's too busy in your career. Don't just be someone who feels sorry for others. Let's become the miracle. God is counting on us. You can lift the fallen. You can heal the hurting. You can be a friend to the lonely. You can help a dream come to pass. You are full of miracles.

Where the Need Is

*"And God will wipe away
every tear from their eyes."*

REVELATION 7:17

One day there will be no more tragedies, no sickness, no more pain. But in the meantime, God is counting on you and me to wipe away those tears. Are you restoring the broken? Are you taking time to help somebody in need? It's great to come to church and celebrate. This is important. But our real assignment begins when we leave the building. Look around and find the discouraged. You may not hear them with your ears, but you can hear them with your heart. You see when somebody is down. All of a sudden you feel that compassion flowing out to them. You think, *I need to go encourage them.* Don't put it off. That's God wanting you to bring healing. There's a tear that needs to be wiped away.

Gracious Words

Gracious words are a honeycomb, sweet to the soul and healing to the bones.

PROVERBS 16:24

We don't always see how powerful we really are. God has put healing in you. Your hugs can cause people to get better. Your kind words can put people back on their feet. A phone call, giving someone a ride, taking them out to dinner, encouraging them in their dreams—there are miracles in you waiting to happen. Some people just need to know that you believe in them and hear you say, "You're amazing! You're going to do great things. I'm praying for you."

What may seem simple and ordinary to you, no big deal, becomes extraordinary when God breathes on it. It can be life-giving. It can be the spark that brings another person back to life. It can help them blossom into all they were created to be.

Hold Them Up

When Moses' hands grew tired...
Aaron and Hur held his hands up—
one on one side, one on the other—
so that his hands remained steady till sunset.

EXODUS 17:12

One time in the Scripture, Moses was on the top of a big hill watching a battle that was taking place. He was holding his rod up in the air. As long as he had his rod up, the Israelites were winning. But every time he put his hands down, the Amalekites would start to win. Finally, Moses was too tired. His brother, Aaron, and a friend named Hur got on each side of Moses, and they held his hands in the air. Because they became the miracle, the Israelites won.

There are people God puts in our path who need us to hold up their hands. They're not going to win by themselves. They need your encouragement and to know that you care. Don't miss the opportunity. Do as Aaron and Hur did and become the miracle.

Serve One Another

"...whoever wishes to become great among you must be your servant, and whoever wishes to be first and most important among you must be slave of all."

MARK 10:43–44 AMP

Back in 2012, a young lady named Meghan was a star long distance runner on her high school track team. At the state track finals, she had already won first place in the 1600-meter race. Next, as she came around the final curve of the 3200-meter race, a girl in front of her collapsed to the ground. What happened next made news around the world. Meghan stopped, picked the girl up, put her arm around her shoulders, and began to carry her toward the finish line.

The people in the stands began to cheer. There wasn't a dry eye in the place. When she got to the finish line, Meghan let her opponent cross first. Meghan said afterward, "Helping her cross that finish line was more satisfying to me than winning the state championship."

Light Will Break Forth

"Then your light will break forth like the dawn, and your healing will quickly appear..."

ISAIAH 58:8

DECEMBER
31

It's great to receive a miracle, but there's no greater feeling than to become a miracle. Who are you carrying? Who are you lifting up? Your destiny is connected to helping others. If you will make it your business to become a miracle, God will make it His business to give you miracles.

You are the answer to somebody's prayer. You can give a rescuing hug this week. You can help a friend cross the finish line. When you go out each day, have this attitude, *I'm a miracle waiting to happen.* If you will live not thinking about how you can get a miracle, but how you can become a miracle, then just as God promised, your light is going to break forth like the dawn. Your healing, your promotion, and your vindication will quickly come.

STAY**CONNECTED,**
BE**BLESSED.**

From thoughtful articles to powerful blogs,
podcasts and more, JoelOsteen.com is full of
inspirations that will give you encouragement and
confidence in your daily life.

AVAILABLE ON JOELOSTEEN.COM

today'sW**O**RD

This daily devotional from Joel
and Victoria will help you grow
in your relationship with the Lord
and equip you to be everything
God intends you to be.

 **Joel Osteen**
STREAMING

Miss a broadcast? Watch Joel
Osteen on demand, and see
Joel LIVE on Sundays.

 Joel Osteen
PODCAST

The podcast is a great way
to listen to Joel where you
want, when you want.

CONNECT WITH US

 Join our
community of
believers on your
favorite social
network.

TAKE HOPE WITH YOU

 Get the inspiration and
encouragement of Joel Osteen
on your iPhone, iPad or Android
device! Our app puts Joel's
messages, devotions and more
at your fingertips.

 Thanks for helping us make a difference in
the lives of millions around the world.

NOTES

NOTES

NOTES